Vocabulary Boosters

Workbook 3

Susan Rogers

Grass Roots Press

Edmonton, Alberta, Canada
2010

Vocabulary Boosters – Workbook 3 © 2010 Grass Roots Press

This book is protected by copyright. All rights reserved. No part of it may be reproduced or transmitted in any form or by any means, electronic, including photocopy, recording, or any information storage and retrieval system, without the prior written permission of the publisher.

Vocabulary Boosters – Workbook 3 is published by

Grass Roots Press
A division of Literacy Services of Canada Ltd.
www.grassrootsbooks.net

AUTHOR	Susan Rogers
EDITORS	Linda Kita-Bradley
	Pat Campbell
	Lisa Zohar
DESIGN	Lara Minja – Lime Design Inc.
LAYOUT	Susan Hunter

ACKNOWLEDGEMENTS

We acknowledge the financial support of the Government of Canada through the Book Publishing Industry Development Program (BPIDP) for our publishing activities.

We acknowledge the support of the Alberta Foundation for the Arts for our publishing programs.

Library and Archives Canada Cataloguing in Publication

Rogers, Susan, 1952-
    Vocabulary boosters / Susan Rogers.

ISBN 978-1-894593-40-3 (bk. 1).--ISBN 978-1-894593-41-0 (bk. 2).--ISBN 978-1-894593-42-7 (bk. 3)

    1. Vocabulary--Problems, exercises, etc. 2. Readers (Adult)
3. Readers for new literates. I. Title.

PE1449.R635 2006   428.1
C2005-904172-2

Contents

About this workbook iv

Lesson	1	Heatstroke	**1**
Lesson	2	Whales on the Beach	**9**
Lesson	3	Lightning Strikes	**17**
Lesson	4	Graffiti	**25**
		Word Search 1	**33**
Lesson	5	Frostbite	**35**
Lesson	6	Caribou	**43**
Lesson	7	San Francisco Earthquake	**51**
Lesson	8	Chocolate	**59**
		Word Search 2	**67**
Lesson	9	Food Allergies	**69**
Lesson	10	Polar Bears	**77**
Lesson	11	Global Warming	**85**
Lesson	12	Extreme Sports	**93**
		Word Search 3	**101**
Lesson	13	Alzheimer's Disease	**103**
Lesson	14	An Australian Pest	**111**
Lesson	15	The Sydney Tar Ponds	**119**
Lesson	16	Identity Theft	**127**
		Word Search 4	**135**
Lesson	17	Diabetes	**137**
Lesson	18	Greyhound Racing	**145**
Lesson	19	Water	**153**
Lesson	20	Body Piercing	**161**
		Word Search 5	**169**
		Glossary	**171**
		Answer Key	**174**

About this workbook

This workbook aims to help adult learners develop their vocabulary through reading passages written at an appropriate level. The workbook is organized around four themes: health, wildlife, the environment, and popular culture. Each lesson presents a non-fiction passage and a set of activities that relate to one of the four themes. Learners can complete the workbook activities independently, with a tutor, or as a group.

In the pre-reading activity, learners activate prior knowledge by brainstorming what they know about the lesson topic. Learners then generate questions about what they would like to learn about the topic. This sets a purpose for reading. After reading the passage, learners reflect upon what they have read and learned by discussing a question that requires drawing information from the passage in order to summarize, supporting an opinion, or making a personal connection to the ideas in the passage.

Learners can use the provided glossary as a (1) preview of the six vocabulary items that will be introduced in the passage or (2) reference as they encounter the new vocabulary in context or while completing the vocabulary activities. Repetition is essential for vocabulary development; consequently, each lesson presents the following five activities that focus on the target vocabulary:

Activity A
Learners figure out the meaning of target vocabulary by reading sentences that contain sufficient context clues to complete the task.

Activity B
Learners are required to make an inference—combine their background knowledge, vocabulary knowledge, and information from the text—in order to complete a sentence.

Activities C & D
Learners deepen their understanding of the target vocabulary by producing the target vocabulary in discussion and writing.

Activity E
Learners work with target vocabulary in different ways to extend their understanding of what the words mean and how they are used.

This workbook also includes the following three features:
    Answer key
    Five word searches
    Twenty idioms

In addition to improving vocabulary, the workbook provides learners with entertaining and informative passages that will help develop reading fluency.

Lesson 1

Health

Heatstroke

Pre-reading Activity

What do you KNOW about heatstroke?	What do you WANT to learn about heatstroke?	What did you LEARN about heatstroke?*

*Complete this column after you read the passage on the next page.

Vocabulary words

fatal prolonged dehydration
replenish excessive underestimate

Heatstroke

Have you ever felt dizzy or weak on a hot summer day? When the temperature soars, we are all at risk from heat exhaustion and heatstroke. Infants, older adults, and people who are obese or who suffer from certain *medical conditions* are at higher risk. Heat exhaustion causes discomfort and pain; heatstroke can be **fatal**. A summer heat wave can cause hundreds of deaths over just a few days.

Prolonged exposure to heat, in combination with **dehydration**, can trigger heat exhaustion. The human body has natural cooling processes, such as sweating, that control body heat. However, in hot and humid weather, these processes may become overloaded and stop working. The body may not be able to release heat, forcing body temperature to rise, sometimes up to 41°C (106°F) or higher. Dehydration worsens the problem. A dehydrated person may not be able to sweat enough to release heat, which also causes body temperature to rise.

> Normal body temperature is 37°C (98.6°F).

The symptoms of heat exhaustion include weakness, fatigue, and dizziness. Muscle cramps may set in. Victims may get a headache or feel sick to their stomach. At the first signs of heat exhaustion, people must get out of the heat and lower their body temperature.

The victim should lie in a cool place with feet raised. Cool water should be applied to the skin and ice packs placed under the armpits and groin. Fanning the victim also helps. The victim should consume slightly salted drinks and avoid coffee and alcohol.

Heat exhaustion can progress to heatstroke with little warning. The victim will develop a fever and act strangely. By this point, the victim has usually stopped sweating. The skin is dry, hot, and red. The pulse is fast and breathing is shallow. The victim may suffer a seizure or go into a coma. Immediate medical assistance is needed.

> Heart disease and high blood pressure are two *medical conditions* that increase the risk of heat exhaustion and heat stroke.

Preventing heat exhaustion and heatstroke is not difficult. Drink plenty of water to **replenish** the body fluids. Wear a hat and loose, light clothing. Stay in the shade and avoid **excessive** exercise when possible. Taking lots of cool showers or baths helps. In prolonged periods of hot weather, spend some time in an air-conditioned place, such as a mall, if possible. A few hours in a cool place gives the body a rest from fighting off the heat. Never leave children or animals inside a car in hot weather.

Most importantly, never **underestimate** how serious heat exhaustion and heatstroke can be.

Discussion

It is not difficult to prevent heat exhaustion or heatstroke. Why do you think some people become victims of these heat-related problems?

Check your understanding

 Circle the best meaning for each bolded word. Try to figure out what the word means by looking at the way it is used in the sentence.

1. Some snakes are so poisonous that their bite is **fatal**. In some cases, a person could die within minutes.
   a. surprising
   b. deadly
   c. painful

2. Scott forgot to water his plants. The plants died of **dehydration**.
   a. the addition of too much water
   b. the hope of finding water
   c. the loss of too much water

3. The employee **replenishes** the grocery shelves once a week.
   a. cleans
   b. refills
   c. changes

4. Pedro's response to my mistake was **excessive**. Later, he apologized.
   a. suitable to the situation
   b. better than what is normal
   c. much more than is expected

5. The weather forecast said there would be a **prolonged** period of rain, so we cancelled our hiking plans for a week.
   a. short
   b. lengthy
   c. wet

6. If a plumber **underestimates** the cost of her labour, she will lose money.
   a. guesses on time
   b. guesses too high
   c. guesses too low

Boost your understanding

 Circle the answer that makes the most sense.

1. It could be **fatal** to
   a. fix a broken chair.
   b. take too much medicine.
   c. eat broccoli every day.

2. They were able to prevent **dehydration** during the long hike. They
   a. had a lot of bug spray with them.
   b. walked quickly through the streams and shallow rivers.
   c. stopped often to drink water.

3. Last week, the rain **replenished** the water in the rain barrels.
   a. There was no rain last week.
   b. Nobody needed rainwater last week.
   c. It rained a lot last week.

4. The noise from the traffic was **excessive**.
   a. I slept like a baby.
   b. I could not sleep.
   c. I could hardly hear the traffic.

5. They went on a **prolonged** trip.
   a. They stayed at a nice hotel.
   b. They were gone for the weekend.
   c. They toured the world.

6. He **underestimated** how much paint he needed.
   a. He was able to finish the paint job.
   b. He had just enough paint to finish.
   c. He had to buy some more paint.

Apply your understanding

C Write an answer for each of the questions. Use complete sentences.

1. Some couples have **prolonged** arguments. Why do some arguments go on and on?
   _____
   _____

2. A mother is shopping with her child. The child keeps grabbing food off the shelves. The mother slaps the child's hand. The child cries. Do you think the mother's punishment is **excessive**? Explain your answer.
   _____
   _____

3. Some people like to do things that can be **fatal**, for example, skydiving. Name two other activities that can be fatal.
   _____
   _____

Complete these sentences using the vocabulary words.

4. After the long walk from downtown, I felt really **dehydrated** so I _____
   _____.

5. During the potluck supper, we had to keep **replenishing** the _____
   because _____.

6. If I drink **excessive** amounts of coffee, I _____
   _____.

Apply your understanding

 **D** Write sentences using the vocabulary words.

fatal _____
_____

prolonged _____
_____

dehydration _____
_____

replenish _____
_____

excessive _____
_____

underestimate _____
_____

"sweating bullets"

The interview was really tough! I was "sweating bullets" by the end of it. I don't think it went very well at all.

"Sweating bullets" means being very anxious and tense.

Extend your understanding

 A prefix is a part of the word that comes before the root word. A prefix has its own meaning.

The prefix **under** has the meaning of not enough or less than necessary.
The word **underestimate** means to estimate less than necessary. For example, he **underestimated** the cost of the paint job.

Complete the sentences with a word from the box. Add **under** to each word before using it in the sentence.

| ~~achieve~~ | develop | fed | employed |
| age | charged | paid | cook |

The first one is an example.

1. Some students **underachieve** because they miss a lot of school due to sickness.

2. This chicken is still raw. Did you _____ it again?

3. She was a doctor in her country before coming to Canada. Now she cleans houses. She is _____ .

4. The teenager couldn't get into the movie because it was rated PG 18. She was _____ .

5. The two cans of tomatoes should have cost $3.29, but I only paid $2.29. I guess the guy at the till _____ me by mistake.

6. Most people feel that they are overworked and _____ .

Lesson 2

Wildlife

Whales on the Beach

Pre-reading Activity

What do you KNOW about whales?	What do you WANT to learn about whales?	What did you LEARN about whales?

* Complete this column after you read the passage on the next page.

Vocabulary words

maintain	stranded	migrate
navigate	composition	ideal

Whales on the Beach

Few things in nature are more tragic than the sight of whales lying helpless on a beach. When local residents spotted 45 whales lying on a remote beach in the northeastern United States, they hurried to save them. Some people covered the whales with cotton sheets to protect their skin from sunburn. Others poured water over the whales to cool them down and **maintain** their body temperatures. At the next high tide, rescuers gently pushed the whales into deeper water. Sadly, the next day, the same whales ended up on another beach. This time efforts to save the **stranded** whales were not successful, and all the whales died.

Every year, stories of stranded whales make the news. Sometimes, a single whale that is sick or injured takes refuge in shallow water. The whale gets trapped by the changing tide and gets stranded on shore. However, marine experts still cannot fully explain why a group of whales ends up stranded on shore at the same time. The experts can only offer possible reasons for this strange animal behaviour.

Whales live in a community called a *pod* and, like humans, have strong social ties to one another. The pod **migrates**, hunts, and shares the care of the young whales, or calves. If one whale suffers from an illness or injury, the other whales usually respond to its distress signals. The healthy whales refuse to abandon a sick or injured pod member and follow it into shallow water.

> A *pod* is a group of ocean animals that are swimming together.

Humans might also cause whale strandings. Whale hunting obviously stresses whales, but even tourist activities such as whale-watching are stressful for these animals. Whaling, or hunting whales, and whale-watching may cause whales to panic and head to shore to escape from humans.

Whales **navigate** by using sonar, a system that uses sound waves to detect underwater objects. Gently sloping coastlines, such as beaches, are hard to detect with sonar, so whales may swim into shallow water by mistake. By the time the whales detect the beach, it may be too late to turn away. Stranding may also occur if whales swim too close to shore while chasing food at low tide.

The greatest danger to stranded whales comes from their bone structure. Whales have fat bodies and light bones. This **composition** is **ideal** for life in the sea, but on land, their body weight crushes their bones. Rescuers are often able to get stranded whales back into deeper water. But the whales sometimes die at sea shortly after because of the damage to their bones.

Why do whales strand themselves? Until experts learn more, the answer to this question will remain one of the big mysteries of the animal kingdom.

Discussion

What other animals have strong social ties to one another?

Check your understanding

 Circle the best meaning for each bolded word. Try to figure out what the word means by looking at the way it is used in the sentence.

1. The locals **maintained** the whale's body temperature by pouring sea water on its skin. They didn't want the whale to get too hot.
   a. heated up; brought to a boiling point
   b. kept at the same level
   c. put in danger by lowering temperature

2. During the flood, people were **stranded** on the roofs of buildings. It took three days for them to be rescued.
   a. drowned very quickly
   b. safe at home
   c. left in a place with no way to leave

3. Whales **migrate** in order to find food. Whales also migrate to avoid extreme temperatures. But they always follow the same routes.
   a. eat lots of fish
   b. move from one area to another
   c. stay in one place to give birth

4. Sailors learn how to **navigate** so that they can cross the ocean from point A to point B.
   a. sing sea songs
   b. tie knots in ropes
   c. find a route to get somewhere

5. The Earth's atmosphere is a **composition** of oxygen, nitrogen, and other gases.
   a. combination of different parts to make a whole
   b. small part of something
   c. something invisible

6. A whale's body is **ideal** for life in the water because it floats easily.
   a. perfect
   b. too big or small
   c. dangerous

Boost your understanding

 Circle the answer that makes the most sense.

1. The long-distance runner couldn't **maintain** his speed because he
   a. got a stomach cramp.
   b. trained very hard.
   c. was running on the track.

2. The man was **stranded** downtown last night.
   a. It was a beautiful, warm night.
   b. The man had no money to get home.
   c. The man was happy to be downtown.

3. Monarch butterflies **migrate** south in the fall. They go as far as Mexico. Monarch butterflies
   a. never leave Mexico.
   b. don't like cold weather.
   c. are born and stay in one place.

4. He wasn't able to **navigate** his way around the city.
   a. It was daytime.
   b. The city was full of many different buildings.
   c. He didn't have a map.

5. The **composition** of the soil was good for growing tomatoes because
   a. the sun shone on it.
   b. it was made up of the right mix of nutrients.
   c. it was brown and crumbly.

6. The dogowners found an **ideal** apartment.
   a. It had a bedroom.
   b. The landlord allowed pets.
   c. The taps were leaking.

Apply your understanding

C Write an answer for each of the questions. Use complete sentences.

1. What can you do if you get **stranded** in a strange place with no money?

   _____
   _____

2. What would be your **ideal** job? Why?

   _____
   _____

3. In what ways do people try to **maintain** their weight?

   _____
   _____

Complete the sentences with your own ideas.

4. The **composition** of the child's painting was interesting. The painting included

   _____.

5. It is hard for pilots to **navigate** when _____
   _____.

6. Animals that live in dry places need to **migrate** so that _____
   _____.

Apply your understanding

 Write sentences using the vocabulary words.

stranded _____
_____

ideal _____
_____

maintain _____
_____

composition _____
_____

navigate _____
_____

migrate _____
_____

"two peas in a pod"

The two brothers do everything together like "two peas in a pod."

Being like "two peas in a pod" means being very similar.

Extend your understanding

The word **pod** has many meanings, but the main meaning of **pod** is connected with the idea of things being in a group.

Pod
a. a group of marine animals, such as whales
b. part of a plant that holds seeds, such as a pea pod
c. a detachable compartment on a spacecraft

 Match the meaning of **pod** in each sentence below with the definitions of **pod** above. Write the letter of the definition in the blank beside the sentence.

The first one is an example.

_b_	1.	The **pod** burst and bits of fluff danced away on the breeze.
___	2.	The boat followed the **pod** for at least 10 kms.
___	3.	The chimp split open the **pod**.
___	4.	The **pod** contained navigation equipment.
___	5.	The scientist crawled into the **pod** for a well-deserved rest.
___	6.	The **pods** are getting smaller due to polluted sea water.

The word **pod** is used to create new words, such as **podcasting** and **Ipod**, which are related to computer technology.

Podcasting is similar to television, except that picture and sound are sent over the Internet instead of to a television. The picture and sound are sent as groups of digital files. An **Ipod** is used to record sound files from the Internet.

Lesson 3

Environment

Lightning Strikes

Pre-reading Activity

What do you KNOW about lightning?	What do you WANT to learn about lightning?	What did you LEARN about lightning?*

* Complete this column after you read the passage on the next page.

Vocabulary words

inspire underrated surge
severe peak conduct

Lightning Strikes

Summer is a time to have fun in the sun. Summer also brings lightning storms—a weather event that can **inspire** awe and fear. While the beauty of lightning can light up a sky, lightning itself can cause massive destruction and death. In North America, lightning strikes start wild fires that cause millions of dollars in damage and kill an average of 80 people every year. Yet lightning is one of the most **underrated** weather hazards.

A bolt of lightning can carry as much as 300,000 volts of electricity. In comparison, most homes have a 220-volt electrical system. If lightning strikes a person, the strong **surge** of electricity can cause heart failure. It can also cause **severe** internal and external burns. People who survive a lightning strike may suffer from long-term problems such as numbness, dizziness, and loss of memory, hearing, and vision.

When thunderclouds appear, knowing when to seek shelter is important. Because light travels faster than sound, you see a lightning bolt before you hear the thunder. To judge how close lightning is, count the seconds between the flash of lightning and the thunderclap. Find shelter if you count 30 seconds or less between lightning and thunder.

Buildings such as shopping malls, schools, and homes are the safest places to wait out a storm. However, keep away from doors and windows. Open structures such as picnic shelters, carports, and porches are not safe. A vehicle provides some protection from lightning. Roll up the windows and do not turn on any electrical devices like the radio or the ignition. Electrical devices can conduct lightning into the vehicle.

If you are outside and cannot reach shelter, stay away from trees and telephone poles. Tall objects attract lightning, and they can fall over during a storm. If you are caught in an open area during a storm, seek shelter in low-lying areas such as ditches. Crouch down and keep your head low, but do not lie on the ground. Stay away from any body of water such as a swimming pool, lake, or even a puddle of water. Lightning is an electric current, which will travel through wet ground and water.

Lightning can travel great distances through power lines. Before a storm **peaks**, disconnect electrical appliances such as radios, TVs, and computers. Do not use anything that can **conduct** electricity, such as stoves or phones, during a lightning storm. Water is an excellent conductor of electricity, so avoid taking a bath or shower during a lightning storm.

An old saying goes that lightning never strikes twice in the same place. Don't believe it. During one storm, lightning hit the Empire State Building eight times within 25 minutes.

Discussion

What is your experience of lightning storms?

Do you love their beauty or fear their danger?

Check your understanding

 Circle the best meaning for each bolded word. Try to figure out what the word means by looking at the way it is used in the sentence.

1. The government predicts that the economy will improve. The good news **inspired** hope among the unemployed.
   a. took away; made impossible to have or own
   b. caused someone to have an emotion or do something
   c. reduced the amount of

2. I loved the movie. I don't know why it's so **underrated**.
   a. having a high value put on it
   b. having a low value put on it
   c. having no value put on it

3. A **surge** of electrical power caused the computer to shut down.
   a. decreasing strength
   b. huge cost
   c. sudden, big increase

4. She suffered **severe** burns from the fire. She needed eight operations to repair the damage to her arms and legs.
   a. small or hard to see
   b. serious or very bad
   c. on the surface

5. Traffic **peaks** during rush hours. Streets usually have less traffic at other times of the day.
   a. reaches highest level
   b. disappears for awhile
   c. moves without problem

6. Styrofoam does not **conduct** heat. That is why coffee shops use Styrofoam cups to serve hot drinks.
   a. allow to pass through
   b. decrease the amount of
   c. block the movement of

Boost your understanding

 Circle the answer that makes the most sense.

1. She was **inspired** after hearing the poet's speech. She went home and
   a. wrote her first poem.
   b. took an aspirin.
   c. made supper.

2. The **underrated** blue team beat the red team. The red team
   a. was afraid to play the blue team.
   b. expected to win.
   c. wanted the blue team to win.

3. A **surge** in the use of electricity might happen when people
   a. turn on air-conditioners during a summer heat wave.
   b. do not pay their electricity bills.
   c. turn off their televisions.

4. She went through a **severe** depression because
   a. she lost her house keys.
   b. she talked to the doctor.
   c. her young son died.

5. The river's water level **peaked** last year when
   a. the river was frozen.
   b. the ice melted.
   c. the rain turned to snow.

6. Metal handles on a pan can **conduct** heat, which means
   a. the pans are safe to use.
   b. the handles stay cool no matter how high the temperature is.
   c. you need to use oven gloves when cooking.

Apply your understanding

C Write an answer for each of the questions. Use complete sentences.

1. Sometimes, a crowd of people **surges** forward like a big wave. When might this happen?

   _____
   _____

2. When do you think athletes normally **peak** in their careers? Why?

   _____
   _____

3. How can parents **inspire** confidence in their children?

   _____
   _____

Complete the sentences with your own ideas.

4. The earthquake was **severe**. It _____.

5. Metal **conducts** electricity so it's not a good idea to _____
   _____.

6. The **underrated** leader of the political party surprised everyone when _____
   _____.

Apply your understanding

 Write sentences using the vocabulary words.

surge _____

_____

peak _____

_____

inspire _____

_____

severe _____

_____

conduct _____

_____

underrated _____

_____

"like greased lightning"

When we opened the front door, our dog got out and ran down the road "like greased lightning."

Moving "like greased lightning" means moving very fast.

Extend your understanding

The word **peak** has many meanings, but the main meaning of **peak** is connected with the idea of coming to a point.

peak
a. the top of a mountain
b. the highest or maximum point
c. reach the maximum or highest point
d. the way something looks when it comes to a point
e. at a period of maximum activity

 Match the meaning of **peak** in each sentence below with the definitions of **peak** above. Write the letter of the definition in the blank beside the sentence.

The first one is an example.

__d__ 1. Beat the whipping cream until it becomes a **peak**.

_____ 2. The actress won an award at the **peak** of her career.

_____ 3. We climbed to the **peak** in six hours.

_____ 4. I try to avoid **peak** travel months. Flights are expensive.

_____ 5. Sales of winter clothes **peak** in December.

Lesson 4

Popular Culture

Graffiti

Pre-reading Activity

What do you KNOW about graffiti?	What do you WANT to learn about graffiti?	What did you LEARN about graffiti?*

* Complete this column after you read the passage on the next page.

Vocabulary words

vandalism	deface	trespass
impression	steep	eradicate

Graffiti

Everyone has seen graffiti on walls, buildings, or other public places. Graffiti is words or drawings that have been scratched, painted, or scribbled, usually without permission. Some people think graffiti is art, but most people view it as **vandalism**.

Graffiti goes back thousands of years. The Romans carved graffiti into stone walls and monuments. In the last century, people carved messages into tree trunks and rocks. Walls, buildings, trains, and road signs are the most common places to see graffiti today. Spray paint and felt-tip markers are the most popular tools.

There are different types of graffiti. One positive type of graffiti comes in the form of colourful pictures, or murals. Building owners or city officials sometimes pay graffiti artists to paint murals on walls or buildings. The murals tell a story or express an idea or feeling.

The most basic form of graffiti is the graffiti artist's personal signature. The signature is a logo or a word that the artist likes. The artist writes the signature in large stylized letters. These words and logos are called tags. Graffiti artists try to paint their tags in as many places as possible.

Fewer graffiti tags appear in cities with lots of murals. Police believe that graffiti artists have their own rules, so one graffiti artist will not paint over or **deface** the work of another graffiti artist. Many cities allow artists to paint murals in the hope of reducing negative types of graffiti.

Gang graffiti is the most negative type of graffiti. Gang members will mark their territory by writing their gang name on public property. These marks are often initials scribbled in a single colour. The marks serve as a warning and a threat to other gangs.

Graffiti artists break laws. Painting on public or private property without permission is illegal. The artists often **trespass** on private property to gain access to a wall, roof, or road sign.

Graffiti can create a bad **impression**. A community with lots of graffiti looks rundown. Pride in the community can suffer. Businesses lose customers. Cities spend thousands of dollars a year to get rid of graffiti. Some cities make the artists pay **steep** fines. People who own businesses need to remove any graffiti that appears on their property. Or they pay a fine too. Other cities have programs to educate youth about the problem of graffiti. In many cities, the citizens work with the police to **eradicate** graffiti. The people report graffiti to the police, and volunteers remove it.

Despite cities' best efforts to control it, graffiti remains a problem.

Discussion

Why do you think people want to write or draw on walls?

Check your understanding

 Circle the best meaning for each bolded word. Try to figure out what the word means by looking at the way it is used in the sentence.

1. In one of the worst acts of **vandalism** this year, angry soccer fans smashed in the windows of hundreds of cars in the downtown area.
   a. damaging property on purpose
   b. playing a sport for fun
   c. fighting with people

2. Out of respect for future users, people should not **deface** library books. They should not write on or highlight the pages.
   a. read for fun
   b. pay for
   c. ruin appearance of

3. The farmer put up a sign in his field that said, "Do not **trespass**." He did not want hunters to shoot deer on his property.
   a. go on private property without permission
   b. destroy crops
   c. pass by without stopping

4. My **impression** of the community was that it seemed unsafe. There was nobody in the streets, and a lot of the streetlights were broken.
   a. interest in
   b. painting of
   c. feeling of

5. The police officer gave me a **steep** fine for throwing garbage on the street. I couldn't pay the fine. I didn't have enough money.
   a. very high
   b. small
   c. strange

6. Scientists worked a long time to **eradicate** smallpox, but finally everyone is safe from this horrible disease.
   a. produce in big amounts
   b. get rid of completely
   c. infect with a disease

Boost your understanding

 Circle the answer that makes the most sense.

1. **Vandalism** upsets people because it
   a. can make the value of property go up.
   b. does not happen enough.
   c. damages things.

2. Last Hallowe'en, a group of kids **defaced** the front doors of many homes in the community. The homeowners decided to
   a. press charges.
   b. sell their houses.
   c. have a street party.

3. A person might **trespass** because he
   a. has a lot of money.
   b. always obeys the law.
   c. wants to take a shortcut.

4. You will make a good **impression** on most people by
   a. talking a lot.
   b. being polite.
   c. having a lot of money.

5. The hillside was quite **steep**. We
   a. found it easy to walk up the hill.
   b. ran all the way up the hill.
   c. were out of breath by the time we made it to the top.

6. Schools are trying to **eradicate**
   a. high grades.
   b. music and art.
   c. bullying.

Apply your understanding

C Write an answer for each of the questions. Use complete sentences.

1. How might a community stop or reduce **vandalism**?
   _____
   _____

2. Describe two ways to make a good **impression** during a job interview.
   _____
   _____

3. Do you think it is possible to **eradicate** poverty? Give a reason for your opinion.
   _____
   _____

Complete the sentences with your own ideas.

4. The kids **defaced** the textbooks by _____.

5. Nobody could **trespass** on the property because the owners _____
   _____.

6. _____ should result in a **steep** punishment.

Apply your understanding

D Write sentences using the vocabulary words.

vandalism _____
_____

impression _____
_____

eradicate _____
_____

deface _____
_____

trespass _____
_____

steep _____
_____

"have down to a fine art"

idiom for today

He "has grocery shopping down to a fine art." He knows where every item in the store is. He knows all the prices. He puts his grocery list in alphabetical order.

"Having something down to a fine art" means being able to do it very well, usually because you have been doing it for a long time.

Extend your understanding

The word **impression** has many meanings.

impression
a. an effect on feeling or mind
b. an effect that is made by putting physical pressure on something
c. a copy of how someone looks or acts

 Match the meaning of **impression** in each sentence below with the definitions of **impression** above. Write the letter of the definition in the blank beside the sentence.

The first one is an example.

___c___ 1. The comedian did a great **impression** of all the famous actors.
_____ 2. My first **impression** of the new boss was not a positive one. He seemed unfair.
_____ 3. The class clown was sent to the principal's office for her insulting **impression** of the teacher.
_____ 4. The fridge left a deep **impression** in the floor.
_____ 5. What was your **impression** of the movie?
_____ 6. The mountains create a lasting **impression** for all visitors.
_____ 7. The actor's **impression** of Gandhi was perfect!

The word **steep** also has many meanings.
a. with a sharp angle going up (a steep hill)
b. very high; almost too much
c. soak in a hot liquid

Read the sentence below. What is the meaning of **steep** in the sentence?

Cities spend many thousands of dollars every year removing graffiti. Some cities impose **steep** fines on the artists.

Word Search 1

L	G	N	W	K	X	A	Q	F	X	J	A	V	S	O	C	M	G
G	U	N	D	E	R	R	A	T	E	D	I	B	D	N	K	I	K
I	D	E	A	L	R	V	A	N	D	A	L	I	S	M	D	G	S
Q	K	U	O	M	R	E	P	L	E	N	I	S	H	P	P	U	O
W	Q	G	O	Y	K	H	K	D	S	T	R	A	N	D	E	D	P
E	S	M	D	P	R	O	L	O	N	G	E	D	P	N	Y	F	W
R	U	N	D	E	R	E	S	T	I	M	A	T	E	T	M	R	Y
A	Z	C	S	U	R	G	E	P	Z	Q	A	I	U	Q	A	H	F
D	U	L	I	T	R	E	S	P	A	S	S	Q	W	B	I	J	A
I	R	G	S	S	N	I	N	S	P	I	R	E	Z	A	N	Q	T
C	C	U	H	A	F	O	X	S	E	V	E	R	E	U	T	W	A
A	D	E	H	Y	D	R	A	T	I	O	N	W	L	I	A	U	L
T	R	E	H	H	X	Q	M	Q	E	X	C	E	S	S	I	V	E
E	E	V	Z	X	G	N	Q	B	A	X	Y	D	U	P	N	K	Q
O	B	M	I	G	R	A	T	E	T	R	M	C	C	E	M	Z	P
N	E	L	E	D	N	H	C	D	W	S	D	E	F	A	C	E	G
Z	T	W	A	Q	B	V	J	E	V	X	G	O	L	K	V	Z	N
N	A	V	I	G	A	T	E	G	T	N	I	O	A	O	L	O	A

deface
inspire
replenish
vandalism

dehydration
maintain
severe
underrated

eradicate
migrate
stranded

excessive
navigate
surge

fatal
peak
trespass

ideal
prolonged
underestimate

Lesson 5

Health

Frostbite

Pre-reading Activity

What do you KNOW about frostbite?	What do you WANT to learn about frostbite?	What did you LEARN about frostbite?*

* Complete this column after you read the passage on the next page.

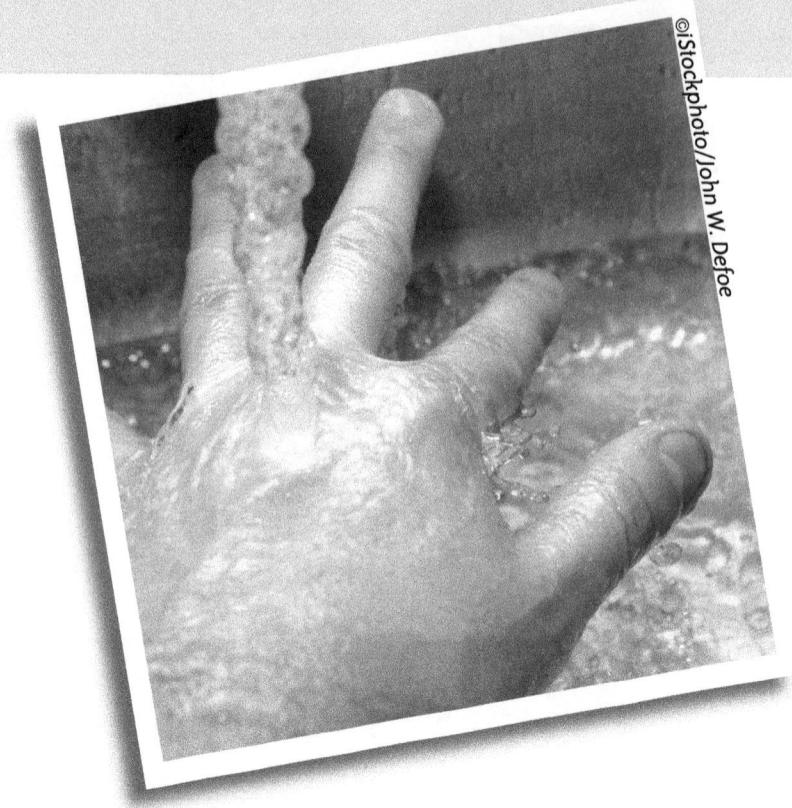

Vocabulary words

constrict	exposed	immerse
gangrene	susceptible	metabolism

Frostbite

Your fingers throb with pain, then lose sensation. The ends of your fingers feel waxy and turn a dark bluish-black. The doctor informs you that your fingertips need to be amputated. You have a case of serious frostbite.

Frostbite is a medical condition caused by prolonged exposure to extreme cold. In cold weather, the skin's blood vessels start to

constrict. The narrow blood vessels reduce the blood flow and the **exposed** skin begins to freeze. The extremities—the fingers, toes, nose, and ears—are especially prone to frostbite.

> Frostbite occurs when the temperature is at or below 0°C (32°F).

In the first stage of frostbite, the frozen skin tingles, burns, or throbs. The skin becomes white and feels stiff. In this stage, it is possible to warm the skin to prevent further damage. The easiest way to warm hands is to place them under the armpits. A frostbitten nose, and ears or toes, can be warmed by covering the area with dry, gloved hands.

In the second stage, the frozen skin loses all sensation and becomes cold, pale, and hard like a block of wood. At this point, the tissue under the skin is frozen as well. If possible, slowly **immerse** the frozen skin in warm—not hot—water. Circulate the water in order to quicken the warming process. Warming frozen skin causes intense pain. As the skin thaws, it may swell, blister, or change colour. After 20 to 30 minutes, the skin should be soft and no longer numb.

In the last stage of frostbite, the skin turns blue or black. **Gangrene** or blood clots may develop. If the frozen area becomes infected, it may need to be amputated. A frostbitten area should not be warmed if there is any chance of the skin freezing again. Keep the area frozen until medical help is available. Do not rub, massage, or put any pressure on the frozen area to try to warm it up. This contact can cause more damage to the area.

Children and seniors are more **susceptible** to extreme cold, so they are more at risk of getting frostbite. The risk of getting frostbite also increases if people have blood vessel damage caused by diabetes, alcohol abuse, or smoking.

To prevent frostbite, dress in loose, light layers that provide ventilation and insulation. The outer layer should be water-resistant. If you are going to be out in the cold for a prolonged period, eat plenty of carbohydrates. Your body's **metabolism** turns the carbohydrates into heat energy. Keep moving in order to stay warm. Frequently check the skin for the danger signs of frostbite.

Discussion

Which jobs put people at risk for frostbite?

Check your understanding

 Circle the best meaning for each bolded word. Try to figure out what the word means by looking at the way it is used in the sentence.

1. One kind of snake kills by **constricting** its prey's lungs. The prey cannot breathe.
   a. eating and spitting out
   b. making bigger by blowing in air
   c. squeezing; making smaller or more narrow

2. I live on an **exposed** part of the island. Sometimes, I feel that the wind will blow my house away.
   a. hidden away
   b. low or underground
   c. not protected; uncovered

3. **Gangrene** occurs when a part of the body stops getting blood. The tissue dies and must be cut off.
   a. something new and healthy
   b. decay of human flesh
   c. a type of pump

4. He **immersed** his shirt in the dye. The shirt turned red in minutes.
   a. put into a liquid so all parts were covered
   b. put under a heavy object to create pressure
   c. put away in a safe place

5. Jose is not getting enough rest. He's not eating well. And it's flu season. He's **susceptible** to colds right now.
   a. protected against; safe from
   b. easily affected by something
   c. being an expert in

6. A person with a high **metabolism** loses weight more easily than a person with a low metabolism.
   a. how the body protects itself from the sun
   b. how the body senses pain
   c. how the body changes food and water into energy

Boost your understanding

 Circle the answer that makes the most sense.

1. The jacket **constricts** my shoulder movements. The jacket is too
   a. small.
   b. big.
   c. fashionable.

2. Walking and jogging boost a person's **metabolism**. Walking and jogging help your body
   a. shrink.
   b. produce energy.
   c. gain weight.

3. His garden was completely **exposed** to the wind. The garden was planted
   a. in an open field.
   b. by a big fence.
   c. under a row of tall trees.

4. **Gangrene** is a serious condition because it can result in
   a. a heart attack.
   b. pregnancy.
   c. a loss of toes or fingers.

5. He **immersed** himself in his work. He
   a. changed jobs all the time.
   b. had a short time to finish a big project.
   c. did not go to work for days.

6. If you are **susceptible** to compliments, it means you
   a. like to compliment others.
   b. don't care what others think about you.
   c. react to compliments that others give you.

Apply your understanding

C Write an answer for each of the questions. Use complete sentences.

1. Some people get **immersed** in activities that they love doing. What activity do you love doing? Why?

   _____
   _____

2. Many teenagers are **susceptible** to peer pressure. Why do teenagers go along with their friends, even when they know they are doing something wrong?

   _____
   _____

3. A person can get **gangrene** from an infected cut or wound. What is one way to keep a wound from getting infected?

   _____
   _____

Complete the sentences with your own ideas.

4. I think my **metabolism** is _____ because my weight _____.

5. When he **exposed** his feelings, she _____
   _____.

6. _____ because her feet were being **constricted**.

Apply your understanding

D Write sentences using the vocabulary words.

immerse _____

_____

susceptible _____

_____

gangrene _____

_____

metabolism _____

_____

exposed _____

_____

constrict _____

_____

"on pins and needles"

I was "on pins and needles" until the doctor phoned with the results.

Being "on pins and needles" means being excited or worried about something.

Extend your understanding

The word **expose** has many meanings.

expose
a. put in a dangerous or harmful position
b. make visible
c. reveal a crime or a fraud, or someone who does wrong
d. introduce someone to something new

(E) Match the meaning of expose in each sentence below with the definitions of expose above. Write the letter of the definition in the blank beside the sentence.

__a__ 1. Eating bad meat **exposes** the dogs to deadly bacteria.

_____ 2. People who do not wear sunblock **expose** their skin to the ultraviolet rays of the sun.

_____ 3. Rubbing the paint away with sandpaper **exposes** the wood.

_____ 4. The parents **exposed** their children to many different types of music.

_____ 5. At the end of the mystery, the author **exposes** the murderer.

_____ 6. Health workers are often **exposed** to diseases.

_____ 7. Our new neighbours **exposed** us to the delicious foods in their culture.

Lesson 6

Wildlife

Caribou

Pre-reading Activity

What do you KNOW about caribou?	What do you WANT to learn about caribou?	What did you LEARN about caribou?*

* Complete this column after you read the passage on the next page.

Vocabulary words

treacherous	vegetation	vulnerable
predator	shadow	frigid

Caribou

Tens of thousands of caribou move like brown rivers across the *tundra* of northern Canada and Alaska. The mighty caribou have begun the migration to their calving grounds—a migration they have made every year since the time of the woolly mammoth.

When the spring snow begins to melt, pregnant cows start moving north to the calving grounds. Here, they will give birth. The cows travel 20 km (12.4 mi) a day for up to two months through deep snow and spring flooding, and over **treacherous** ice. The cows arrive at the calving grounds weak, exhausted, and hungry. Weeks later, the rest of the herd follows.

The calving grounds along the Arctic coastal plains provide the caribou herd with nutritious **vegetation** such as *lichen* and moss. The cows need the nutrition to produce the rich milk that their calves depend on. The cool breezes from the Arctic Ocean provide the caribou with relief from biting black flies and mosquitoes.

> *Lichen* is a type of small plant that grows on rocks.

Caribou mothers give birth to a single calf. The calves are most **vulnerable** right after birth. The cows choose calving grounds that are as safe as possible from **predators** such as wolves and grizzly bears. About 25 percent of the calves still die due to predators and natural hazards such as storms.

In summer, the caribou herds move over the tundra looking for vegetation. The caribou try to avoid the growing number of biting insects by climbing up mountains and to the tops of ridges. At times, the black flies and mosquitoes harass the caribou to the point that they cannot feed. Some caribou grow weak and die.

> *Tundra* is a large area of flat land where there are no trees and the ground is always frozen.

In autumn, the falling temperatures and snow force the caribou off the tundra. The herd must return south. During this part of the migration, caribou grow antlers to prepare for the rut, or breeding season. The bulls' antlers are weapons for fighting with other bulls. The winning bulls mate with the cows. But fighting can tire the bulls, making them easy prey for the wolves and bears that constantly **shadow** the herd.

Caribou spend the dark, **frigid** months of winter in the protection of forested areas. The snow is softer and less deep, so the caribou can reach the lichen, moss, and grass. In milder winters, caribou are able to recover their strength. The cows are no longer nursing their calves, the bulls are no longer fighting, and the biting insects have disappeared.

When the spring snow begins to melt, the cows will once again begin to move north. And once again the caribou herds will complete the 2,000 to 3,000 km migration to the calving grounds and back again—as regular as time.

Discussion

What hardships do caribou face during migration?

Check your understanding

 Circle the best meaning for each bolded word. Try to figure out what the word means by looking at the way it is used in the sentence.

1. Crossing the old wooden bridge was **treacherous**. The bridge creaked and swayed from side to side in the wind.
    a. easy and fast
    b. full of dangers
    c. impossible

2. Deserts have very little **vegetation** compared to thick, green jungles.
    a. plant life
    b. sand
    c. open areas

3. The soldiers were **vulnerable** as they crossed an open field in enemy territory.
    a. safe and sound
    b. invisible
    c. open to danger

4. Mice have a lot of natural **predators** including hawks, snakes, and cats. But there still seem to be a lot of mice around.
    a. animals that eat leaves and berries
    b. animals that fly
    c. animals that live by killing and eating other animals

5. A private detective will often **shadow** people to find out where they go. The people do not know the detective is near them.
    a. follow and watch closely
    b. pay off secretly
    c. shout loudly at

6. In the Arctic, people cope with **frigid** weather by wearing fur coats.
    a. extremely wet
    b. extremely cold
    c. extremely warm

Boost your understanding

 Circle the answer that makes the most sense.

1. The side roads were **treacherous** after the ice storm.
   a. Cars were getting stuck on the side roads.
   b. City crews quickly cleared the side roads of ice.
   c. The ice storm did not cause much damage.

2. It was difficult to get through the thick **vegetation**
   a. in the city.
   b. in the forest.
   c. in the sky.

3. The cat was **vulnerable** in the outdoors. The cat
   a. was a good hunter.
   b. was wild.
   c. had no claws.

4. The **predator** watched as the lizard moved closer. The predator was a
   a. snake.
   b. bug.
   c. zebra.

5. Wolves **shadow** their prey because they
   a. are waiting for the right time to attack.
   b. like to scare animals.
   c. do not know where the prey is.

6. Animals that are able to live in **frigid** weather are
   a. elephants and giraffes.
   b. polar bears and penguins.
   c. camels and lizards.

Apply your understanding

C Write an answer for each of the questions. Use complete sentences.

1. What kinds of animals, including birds and insects, live in your community? Which of these animals are **predators**?

   _____

   _____

2. Why do people sometimes feel **vulnerable** when the economy is bad?

   _____

   _____

3. Some parts of big cities do not have much **vegetation**. Is it important to have vegetation in your environment? Why or why not?

   _____

   _____

Complete the sentences with your own ideas.

4. Because of the constant **frigid** temperatures all winter, _____

   _____ .

5. The first day on the job, I **shadowed** my co-worker because _____

   _____ .

6. The river was **treacherous**. It _____ .

Apply your understanding

 Write sentences using the vocabulary words.

predator _____
_____

vulnerable _____
_____

vegetation _____
_____

frigid _____
_____

shadow _____
_____

treacherous _____
_____

"a fly on the wall"

I'd give anything to be "a fly on the wall" when the boss reads my email.

Wanting to be "a fly on the wall" means wanting to be somewhere secretly to see and hear what happens.

Extend your understanding

The word **shadow** has many meanings.

shadow
- a. follow and watch closely without being seen
- b. an area of shade caused by something blocking the light
- c. a small degree of; a trace of
- d. a close or constant companion
- e. something that causes sadness or gloom
- f. look like something, but just a little

 Match the meaning of **shadow** in each sentence below with the definitions of **shadow** above. Write the letter of the definition in the blank beside the sentence.

The first one is an example.

__f__ 1. Since the politician lost the election, she has been a **shadow** of her former self.

____ 2. I couldn't tell if he was crying. His face was in **shadow**.

____ 3. The police officer **shadowed** the drug dealer.

____ 4. Her younger sister was her **shadow**.

____ 5. The child's illness cast a **shadow** over her family's happiness.

____ 6. The answer to her question caused just a **shadow** of doubt to cross her face.

____ 7. He was so sulky and miserable. He cast a **shadow** on what should have been a happy day.

Lesson 7

Environment

San Francisco Earthquake

Pre-reading Activity

What do you KNOW about the San Francisco Earthquake?	What do you WANT to learn about the San Francisco Earthquake?	What did you LEARN about the San Francisco Earthquake?*

*Complete this column after you read the passage on the next page.

Vocabulary words

corrupt	shatter	devastation
chaos	loot	extinguish

San Francisco Earthquake

In the early years of the twentieth century, San Francisco was already a major port city with 400,000 people. It was known for its wealth, architecture, and culture. At the same time, San Francisco was a wild town full of criminals, con men, and **corrupt** politicians. Crime and shady deals were a part of life in the brothels, gambling houses, and opium halls. On April 18, 1906, an underground shock rumbled beneath the entire city. What happened next would affect the lives of rich and poor, good and bad.

About 25 seconds after the first underground shock hit San Francisco, a powerful earthquake rocked San Francisco for over 45 seconds. Buildings collapsed and windows **shattered**. People were thrown from their beds. Others were buried under tons of stone, iron, and bricks. Heavy objects flew though the air. But the **devastation** had only just begun.

Fires broke out everywhere in the city because of broken gas mains. The earthquake had also destroyed water lines, cutting the water supply to the firefighters. Firefighters worked bravely, but the flames spread out of control. The desperate firefighters used dynamite to blow up buildings in order to create open spaces. The firefighters hoped that the open spaces would stop the fires spreading from building to building.

The city was in **chaos**. In an attempt to escape from the fires, terrified people ran for the hills surrounding the city. Injured and dying victims were pulled along the burning streets on blankets. Some people took advantage of the confusion. They began to riot and **loot** businesses and homes not yet destroyed by fire. The mayor eventually ordered the police to shoot any rioters or looters.

After four days, the firefighters managed to **extinguish** the fires. But 80 percent of the city had burned to the ground. The fires had caused more deaths and damage than the earthquake itself. The official death count was listed as 700. But some say as many as 3,000 people died in the disaster, and 225,000 were left homeless.

The great San Francisco earthquake and fire of 1906 was one of the world's first natural disasters to be photographed. Consequently, the devastating scenes are still alive in people's memories. Will another earthquake of this *magnitude* hit San Francisco? San Francisco is located in one of the most dangerous earthquake zones in the world. Many people believe getting hit again is just a matter of time.

> Magnitude is a number that shows the power of an earthquake. For example, an earthquake with magnitude 5 is 10 times stronger than an earthquake with magnitude 4.

Discussion

We see a person's true character in times of trouble. Do you think this is true? Why or why not?

Check your understanding

 Circle the best meaning for each bolded word. Try to figure out what the word means by looking at the way it is used in the sentence.

1. Criminals run the brothels. They pay off the **corrupt** mayor so he won't shut the brothels down.
   a. honest and moral
   b. without moral beliefs
   c. not very smart

2. During the earthquake, the windows in the buildings **shattered**. The flying glass injured hundreds of people.
   a. cracked in two or three places
   b. became dirty and full of dust
   c. broke into many little pieces

3. **Devastation** was everywhere after the disaster. Ruined buildings. Collapsed bridges. Roads ripped up and washed away.
   a. groups of people who help
   b. signs of life
   c. almost complete destruction

4. Some people ran blindly through the streets. Others started to riot. The police could do nothing as the **chaos** became worse.
   a. complete confusion
   b. darkness
   c. rules and laws

5. Some people started to **loot** during the riot. They broke the windows of small shops. They carried away food, jewellery, and clothing.
   a. steal things that only rich people have
   b. steal things because of hunger
   c. steal things in a situation of confusion

6. Firefighters could not **extinguish** the fires because they had no water.
   a. put out
   b. add fuel to
   c. protect or save

Boost your understanding

 Circle the answer that makes the most sense.

1. **Corrupt** leaders in a city cause problems because the people
   a. can't trust the leaders to be honest.
   b. don't like to live in an ugly city.
   c. need jobs and good housing.

2. She **shattered** his heart when she said,
   a. "I'm mad at you."
   b. "I'm leaving."
   c. "I love you."

3. Experts are trying to figure out what is causing the **devastation** of oak trees.
   a. Oak trees are dying.
   b. There are too many oak trees.
   c. Oak trees are growing in strange places.

4. Which of the following is most likely to cause **chaos** on a crowded street?
   a. gunshots
   b. a motorcycle
   c. traffic lights

5. Some people in the city **looted** as much as they could. The city had
   a. spent a lot of money on putting plants in public places.
   b. started to support more public transportation.
   c. suffered a major blackout.

6. He **extinguished** the candle before leaving the room.
   a. He left the candle in a safe place.
   b. The candle continued to burn.
   c. The candle would not burn his home down.

Apply your understanding

C Write an answer for each of the questions. Use complete sentences.

1. Why do you think some people become **corrupt** after they enter politics?

   _____

   _____

2. An earthquake is a natural hazard that can cause great **devastation**. What other natural hazards cause devastation?

   _____

   _____

3. People go through times of **chaos** in their lives. What is one thing that causes **chaos** in a person's life?

   _____

   _____

Complete the sentences with your own ideas.

4. The peaceful protest turned into an ugly riot. Rioters started **looting** and _____.

5. _____ is one way to **extinguish** a fire that starts in a frying pan full of oil.

6. _____. And that's why it **shattered**.

Apply your understanding

 **D** Write sentences using the vocabulary words.

corrupt _____
_____

devastation _____
_____

chaos _____
_____

loot _____
_____

extinguish _____
_____

shatter _____
_____

"play with fire"

She's seeing a married man. She's "playing with fire."

"Playing with fire" means being involved in an activity that could be dangerous or cause problems.

Extend your understanding

Many words have base words. New words can be built from a base word by adding suffixes. For example, suffixes can be added to the base word **corrupt** to build the new words **corrupts**, **corrupted**, and **corruption**.

 Build new words from the base words.
Then use the base word or one of the new words you built in a sentence.

The first one is an example.

corrupt: *corrupts* *corrupted* *corrupting* *corruption*
The young girl was corrupted by the gang members.

shatter: _____

loot: _____

devastate: _____

extinguish: _____

Lesson 8

Popular Culture

Chocolate

Pre-reading Activity

What do you KNOW about chocolate?	What do you WANT to learn about chocolate?	What did you LEARN about chocolate?*

*Complete this column after you read the passage on the next page.

Vocabulary words

seductive	fret	crave
currency	status symbol	global

Chocolate

Chocolate is one of the most satisfying foods we know. Yet we have mixed feelings about this **seductive** treat. We love chocolate, but we also **fret** over eating too much of it. Chocolate is often the first thing we avoid when we diet, but it is also the first thing we reach for when we need a sugar fix. Studies suggest that chocolate is good for us in some ways, but nobody knows for sure just how good. One thing is certain—people have been **craving** chocolate for centuries.

Chocolate is made from the beans of cacao fruit, which comes from the cacao tree. The cacao tree is native to Central and South America. The tasty secret of the cacao tree was discovered about 3,000 years ago. An ancient group of people in Central America used the fruit to make an alcoholic drink.

About 500 years later, ancient peoples of Mexico were using cacao beans. They used the beans as a cure for stomach problems and to increase sex drive. The beans were crushed and pounded to make a bitter drink. The drink was flavoured with local ingredients like honey, dried flowers, and vanilla.

Cacao beans were believed to be the food of the gods. Rulers and priests drank cacao-based drinks from gold cups during special ceremonies. Apparently, one *Aztec* ruler drank up to 50 cups of cacao a day. Cacao beans were also used as local **currency**. Three beans bought one fresh avocado. One hundred beans bought a turkey.

> The *Aztecs* were an ancient people who lived in Mexico.

Cacao beans reached Europe in the 16th century. In 1502, a European explorer named Christopher Columbus came across a canoe filled with goods for trade—including cacao beans. He brought the beans back to Spain, but the king and queen were not impressed. The beans tasted too bitter. In time, the Spaniards recognized the value of the cacao bean. The bitter flavour of cacao-bean drinks was sweetened with sugar. By the 17th century, drinking chocolate had become a **status symbol**. In England, chocolate houses served chocolate drinks to people who could afford it. It was not until the mid 1800s that chocolate drinks became the chocolate bar we eat today.

Chocolate is now a **global** business. Six companies control 80 percent of the chocolate that is bought and sold worldwide. The six companies include Nestlé, Mars, Hershey's, and Kraft. These four companies alone sell over $25 billion worth of chocolate every year. Sadly, the people who grow, pick, and prepare cacao beans see very little of this money.

The next time you bite off a piece of your favourite chocolate bar, stop a moment and remember—this food of the gods has a long, rich history.

Discussion

Do you think chocolate deserves to be called the food of the gods? Why or why not?

Check your understanding

 Circle the best meaning for each bolded word. Try to figure out what the word means by looking at the way it is used in the sentence.

1. Chocolate is **seductive**. Many people cannot stop eating it for some reason.
   a. cheap and easy to find
   b. tempting; very attractive
   c. not interesting or boring

2. Don't **fret** over the weather. What's the use? The weather is out of your control.
   a. worry about
   b. forget about
   c. be happy about

3. Some people **crave** licorice. They will make a special trip to the store just to buy some.
   a. have a strong wish for
   b. really dislike
   c. make at home by hand

4. Canadians and Americans use dollars. The British use pounds. Mexicans use pesos. There are many different kinds of **currency** in the world.
   a. countries
   b. people
   c. money

5. Flying in your own jet is a **status symbol**. Only millionaires can afford such a thing.
   a. something that shows if a person likes flying
   b. something that shows a person's high level in society
   c. something that shows how cheap things are

6. Climate change is a **global** concern. Countries all over the world will be affected in some way.
   a. local
   b. around the world
   c. not important

Boost your understanding

 Circle the answer that makes the most sense.

1. People might be **seductive** when they are trying to
   a. get a child to eat vegetables.
   b. get the attention of someone they like.
   c. entertain their family.

2. I **fret** every time I get into the car with my friend.
   a. I don't feel safe when my friend drives.
   b. My friend has had her driver's licence for years.
   c. I like to make my friend laugh while she is driving.

3. If you **crave** time alone, you
   a. like to spend all your time with other people.
   b. are bored when you are by yourself.
   c. probably do not get enough time alone.

4. Some groups of people used shells as **currency**. These people
   a. did not want shells.
   b. thought shells were important.
   c. were poor.

5. The people in my society consider cabbage a **status symbol** because cabbage is
   a. hard to get.
   b. common.
   c. healthy.

6. Cell phones are **global**.
   a. Travellers can use cell phones in many countries.
   b. Cell phones are rare and hard to find.
   c. Only North Americans have cell phones.

Apply your understanding

 Write an answer for each of the questions. Use complete sentences.

1. Many non-verbal behaviours express emotions. Many of these behaviours are **global**. For example, smiling is a global expression of happiness. Name one other behaviour that is probably global.

   _____
   _____

2. Why do you think some people are into **status symbols**?

   _____
   _____

3. Some people **fret** over being late. Others worry about the environment. What makes you fret? Explain why.

   _____
   _____

Complete the sentences with your own ideas.

4. I think a **seductive** person is a person who _____
   _____.

5. I **crave** _____ when _____
   _____.

6. I wish _____ was a form of **currency** because I have a lot of it.

64 Popular Culture Vocabulary Boosters Workbook 3

Apply your understanding

 Write sentences using the vocabulary words.

global _____

_____

status symbol _____

_____

fret _____

_____

seductive _____

_____

crave _____

_____

currency _____

_____

"spill the beans"

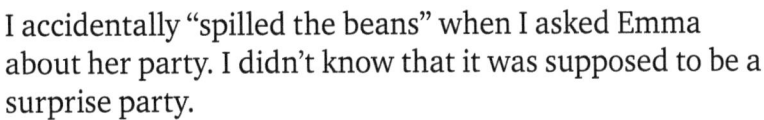

I accidentally "spilled the beans" when I asked Emma about her party. I didn't know that it was supposed to be a surprise party.

"Spilling the beans" means giving away a secret or a surprise.

Extend your understanding

A **status symbol** is a sign of a person's position or level in society. Status symbols are often related to what a society values. So status symbols differ from society to society. North American society values money. Therefore, expensive homes, designer clothing, and luxury cars are status symbols in North American society.

Status symbols change over time. For example, a long time ago, books were a status symbol. Very few people had access to books because books were rare. But today, many people have access to books, so books are no longer a status symbol.

 Read the descriptions of society A, B, and C. Then choose a status symbol from the box that each society might value. Give a reason for your answer.

Society A
This society is tough. It values bravery and honour. The greatest honour is to fight and die for the people.

Society B
Most people work hard to survive. They spend many hours a day under a hot sun working in their fields. They have just enough to eat.

Society C
Most people work long hours every day. They get little time off. They spend most of their time indoors because of the cold climate.

Status Symbols

a suntan	a big scar	a long vacation in Mexico
soft skin	being overweight	a medal of courage

Word Search 2

U	Y	M	D	E	V	A	S	T	A	T	I	O	N	R	E	E	A
T	U	X	T	S	E	D	U	C	T	I	V	E	P	J	B	B	Z
K	R	X	V	U	L	N	E	R	A	B	L	E	U	S	E	K	A
T	T	W	I	F	P	J	Z	S	H	A	T	T	E	R	I	H	S
D	V	H	Q	K	C	B	C	U	R	R	E	N	C	Y	E	D	T
P	Z	C	F	Q	C	H	A	O	S	N	C	O	R	R	U	P	T
S	R	E	R	M	E	T	A	B	O	L	I	S	M	M	Q	R	C
D	T	E	X	I	V	J	D	I	P	F	R	I	G	I	D	H	X
X	F	A	D	P	U	G	T	T	P	G	Q	J	M	Q	S	C	F
J	U	U	T	A	O	A	S	U	S	C	E	P	T	I	B	L	E
W	T	O	L	U	T	S	J	A	Z	D	R	V	U	Q	S	C	G
F	O	D	I	E	S	O	E	Y	N	F	O	G	F	C	V	H	A
L	I	O	G	U	M	S	R	D	V	P	N	A	T	L	S	N	N
X	L	E	F	Q	F	Z	Y	U	I	I	M	M	E	R	S	E	G
F	V	H	P	T	Q	L	B	M	T	V	V	X	M	P	S	L	R
S	V	H	H	D	D	S	Q	X	B	I	J	O	Q	Q	Q	Y	E
I	N	Q	K	B	S	Q	E	K	G	O	H	X	X	P	D	E	N
F	R	E	T	M	I	Z	K	A	J	G	L	O	B	A	L	O	E

chaos corrupt currency devastation exposed extinguish
frigid gangrene global immerse fret loot
metabolism predator seductive shatter status symbol susceptible
vegetation vulnerable

Lesson 9

Health

Food Allergies

Pre-reading Activity

What do you KNOW about food allergies?	What do you WANT to learn about food allergies?	What did you LEARN about food allergies?*

*Complete this column after you read the passage on the next page.

Vocabulary words

rapidly	cautious	scrutinize
trace	vigilant	adrenaline

Food Allergies

Over the past decade, food allergies have been increasing, especially among children. Eight foods make up 90 percent of all food allergies. These foods are peanuts, tree nuts, milk, eggs, soy, wheat, fish, and shellfish. For a small percentage of people, eating one of these eight foods could lead to death.

At some time in their lives, most people have a bad reaction to something they eat or drink. They may experience symptoms such as stomach cramps, diarrhea, or vomiting. These symptoms are usually due to a food intolerance, rather than a food allergy. For example, if people lack the enzyme needed to digest milk products, they may experience lactose intolerance. Allergic reactions are much more serious than a reaction caused by food intolerance.

Allergic reactions can begin **rapidly**—from only minutes to just two hours after exposure to the food. Symptoms can range from mild reactions such as a tingling sensation in the mouth to more dangerous reactions such as a swollen tongue or throat. The swelling may affect the victim's ability to breathe or swallow. Itchy red skin or hives are a common allergic reaction. In rare cases, a victim may lose consciousness, go into a coma, or even die.

In recent years, nut allergies have received a lot of attention. Many schools have banned nuts or created nut-free zones. Some restaurant menus indicate which dishes contain nuts. Most airlines no longer serve nuts as snacks. Some experts believe that the public is over-reacting to the news it hears about nut allergies. Whether or not the public is over-reacting, the fact is people with severe nut allergies must be **cautious** as to what they eat.

People who are allergic to peanuts **scrutinize** food labels and look for warnings like "may contain nuts." When they eat out, they ask about food preparation and ingredients. Just a **trace** of peanuts on utensils or countertops can trigger an allergic reaction.

Parents of children with a nut allergy always need to be **vigilant**. They must train their children not to share or trade food with friends, and to tell people about their allergy. Parents must also be aware of how to treat their children in case of an allergy attack. Using an injection of **adrenaline** is the most common treatment for a severe allergic reaction.

Nobody knows for sure why more and more people are developing food allergies. Some of the possible reasons are new chemicals in our foods, too much stress, poor diet, and genetics. Whatever the reason, people with the most serious food allergies know that fatal consequences could be just a peanut away.

Discussion

Do you think it is a good idea to ban children from bringing nuts to school? Why or why not?

Check your understanding

 Circle the best meaning for each bolded word. Try to figure out what the word means by looking at the way it is used in the sentence.

1. The tenants got out of the building as **rapidly** as possible. The fire was spreading from apartment to apartment.
    a. quietly
    b. annoyingly
    c. quickly

2. The **cautious** lion tamer entered the cage slowly. She knew the lions were tame, but she also knew the lions could turn on her at any time.
    a. fast
    b. careful
    c. sad

3. She **scrutinized** the second-hand car before she bought it. She checked out every part of the car. Then she took it for a test drive.
    a. quickly cleaned
    b. damaged
    c. examined carefully

4. The crime unit checked out the whole apartment. They could find no **trace** of drugs. They left without making an arrest.
    a. very tiny amount
    b. big pile
    c. variety

5. Crossing guards must be **vigilant** at all times. They are responsible for making sure that school children get across busy streets safely.
    a. alert and watchful
    b. relaxed
    c. angry

6. Our bodies produce **adrenaline** when we are very excited or frightened.
    a. something that makes the heart beat faster
    b. something that helps the stomach digest food
    c. something that helps the body grow

Boost your understanding

 Circle the answer that makes the most sense.

1. He **rapidly** filled the cart with groceries.
   a. The store was closing in five minutes.
   b. One of the wheels on the cart was broken.
   c. He had a short grocery list.

2. The **cautious** drivers paid attention to the signs. The road was
   a. clear of traffic.
   b. under construction.
   c. newly paved.

3. He **scrutinized** every word. He was reading
   a. a phone book.
   b. his father's will.
   c. a funny story.

4. The injury left a **trace** of a scar on her arm.
   a. The injury healed well.
   b. She always kept her arm hidden from view.
   c. The scar was on the inside of her arm.

5. If you are **vigilant** about being safe in your home, you would likely
   a. keep your door locked.
   b. leave a key in the mailbox.
   c. leave your door unlocked.

6. She felt the **adrenaline** running through her body. She was
   a. sleeping deeply.
   b. laughing very hard at a joke.
   c. stuck in an elevator all alone.

Apply your understanding

C Write an answer for each of the questions. Use complete sentences.

1. When was the last time you could feel **adrenaline** racing through your body? Describe the situation.

   _____
   _____

2. A child gets lost on a school trip. The school bans field trips. Do you agree with this policy? Or is it up to teachers to be more **vigilant**?

   _____
   _____

3. It is normal for water to have **traces** of some bacteria in it. However, some bacteria are dangerous. Who controls the quality of water in your community?

   _____
   _____

Complete the sentences with your own ideas.

4. Being **cautious** is a good idea when _____
   _____.

5. She could hear her boss coming down the hall, so she **rapidly** _____
   _____.

6. The detective **scrutinized** every inch of the abandoned car. He _____
   _____.

Apply your understanding

 Write sentences using the vocabulary words.

adrenaline _____
_____

vigilant _____
_____

trace _____
_____

cautious _____
_____

rapidly _____
_____

scrutinize _____
_____

"smells fishy"

Something "smells fishy" about her story. She said she went to bed early, but I know for a fact that she worked late that night.

If a situation "smells fishy," it means that the situation seems suspicious, or you do not believe what someone is telling you.

Extend your understanding

The word **trace** has many meanings.

trace
a. a very small amount
b. a mark that is left by passing animals, people, or vehicles; evidence
c. follow the trail of; track down
d. copy a drawing by marking lines on transparent paper laid on the drawing

 Match the meaning of **trace** in each sentence below with the definitions of **trace** above. Write the letter of the definition in the blank beside the sentence.

The first one is an example.

____c____ 1. The police used dogs to **trace** the escaped convicts.
_____ 2. I can't draw, so I usually **trace** pictures.
_____ 3. The house inspector said there were **traces** of asbestos in the basement.
_____ 4. The hunter spent days looking for **traces** of moose.
_____ 5. I want to **trace** my family history.

The word **rapid** also has different meanings.
a. quick
b. place in a stream or river where water flows very fast, usually because of rocks

Read the sentence below. What are the meanings of **rapid**?

Getting through the **rapids** at a **rapid** pace was impossible. The canoe kept bumping and scraping against the rocks.

Lesson 10

Wildlife

Polar Bears

Pre-reading Activity

What do you KNOW about polar bears?	What do you WANT to learn about polar bears?	What did you LEARN about polar bears?*

* Complete this column after you read the passage on the next page.

Vocabulary words

image	inhospitable	acute
vicinity	species	apathy

Polar Bears

Think of the Arctic and an **image** comes to mind—the polar bear. For future generations, this symbol of the north might only be a memory. Scientists who study the Arctic believe two-thirds of polar bears could disappear by 2050. Global warming threatens to push the polar bear to extinction.

Polar bears have many unique adaptations for living in the Arctic's

inhospitable climate. Their skin is black, which helps them absorb as much heat as possible. Under the skin, a layer of blubber up to 10 cm (4 in) thick provides insulation. Two coats of fur provide further protection from the bitter cold. Polar bears depend on the cold temperatures and arctic ice to survive. They could not survive in warmer climates or habitats. But global warming is putting polar bears to the test.

Polar bears are excellent hunters, with an **acute** sense of smell. Their diet consists mostly of seals, which the polar bears hunt in the spring and summer. Their keen sense of smell helps polar bears detect prey up to a kilometre away. The pads on the bottoms of their feet have small bumps that provide traction on ice while tracking prey. Strong, powerful claws enable polar bears to catch and hold their prey.

The main habitat of the polar bear, especially during the long winter months, is on top of the ice that covers the arctic seas. Polar bears live on huge floating platforms of sea ice called ice floes. The bears hunt seals by catching the seals as they come up and breathe through holes in the thick ice floes. As global warming melts the ice, polar bears have fewer stable ice floes on which to hunt. Reports of polar bear drownings are increasing. The bears get caught in the open sea and die of exhaustion as they try to swim to land.

Global warming means polar bears are losing their most important habitat. Ice floes are melting earlier in the spring and polar bears have less time to hunt and fatten up on seals. Polar bears will eat fish, small animals, birds, and plants, but they need the calorie-rich blubber and skin of seals to survive. Sometimes, hungry polar bears looking for food will wander into the **vicinity** of communities. If a community feels threatened, the residents will often respond by shooting the polar bears.

Polar bears are adapted to and have survived in one of the harshest climates on Earth. They have no natural predators. But they do have a man-made predator—global warming. As humans, we need to recognize the importance of sharing the planet with other **species**. To see the polar bear die off because of human **apathy** would be a tragedy.

Discussion

What can humans do to save the polar bear?

Check your understanding

 Circle the best meaning for each bolded word. Try to figure out what the word means by looking at the way it is used in the sentence.

1. When I was young, I had an **image** of what my life would be like as an adult. Things have turned out very differently.
   a. photo or video
   b. mental picture
   c. history in writing

2. Deserts can seem **inhospitable** to people who are not used to living in a hot and dry climate.
   a. busy; full of life
   b. far away
   c. hard to live or survive in

3. An eagle's eyesight is more **acute** than a human's. An eagle can see about six times better than a person.
   a. sensitive
   b. limited
   c. easy to notice

4. Parents like to live in the **vicinity** of a school so that their children do not have to take a bus every day.
   a. inside or centre
   b. area close to or around a place
   c. area that is far away

5. The beluga whale lives in the St. Lawrence River. This **species** of whale is fighting for survival in the busy, polluted river.
   a. group of animals that can breed with one another
   b. path of waterways that leads to the sea
   c. regulations and laws that protect animals

6. Very few people turned out to support the home team. The people's **apathy** is cause for worry.
   a. lack of money
   b. lack of skill
   c. lack of interest

Boost your understanding

 Circle the answer that makes the most sense.

1. I have only an **image** of the sea. I
    a. am afraid to swim in the sea.
    b. live on the sea.
    c. have never been to the sea.

2. They biked in some **inhospitable** areas. They biked
    a. along country roads.
    b. through swampland.
    c. across a bridge.

3. His hearing is **acute**.
    a. He is a good-looking guy.
    b. Be careful of what you say around him.
    c. Speak up when you want to talk to him.

4. I live in the **vicinity** of downtown. I
    a. have to take a long bus ride downtown.
    b. live in a two-bedroom apartment.
    c. can walk downtown in 10 minutes.

5. There are 17 **species** of penguins in the world. There are
    a. 17 penguins in the world.
    b. 17 different types of penguins in the world.
    c. 17 special penguins in the world.

6. She is getting married tomorrow. She feels nothing but **apathy**. She
    a. cannot afford to go to Europe on her honeymoon.
    b. is making sure every detail is taken care of.
    c. is in love with her best friend's husband.

Apply your understanding

C Write an answer for each of the questions. Use complete sentences.

1. Some people do not vote because they feel a sense of **apathy**. Why do some people not care about politics or voting?

   _____
   _____

2. Many **species** of insects live in forests. Many species of insects are dying off. Why do you think insect life in forests is dying off?

   _____
   _____

3. Many teenage girls today suffer from a negative body **image**. They believe that they are overweight even if their body weight is normal. How can parents help their teenagers develop a positive body image?

   _____
   _____

Complete the sentences with your own ideas.

4. They chose an **inhospitable** area of the country to live in. The worst part about the area is _____.

5. Superheroes have **acute** powers. For example, _____
   _____.

6. They live in the **vicinity** of a _____. They hear nothing but noise night and day.

Apply your understanding

 Write sentences using the vocabulary words.

apathy _____

_____

species _____

_____

image _____

_____

inhospitable _____

_____

acute _____

_____

vicinity _____

_____

"grin and bear it"

My brother-in-law is quite rude, but what can I do? He's family. I just have to "grin and bear it."

"Grin and bear it" means to tolerate something unpleasant, but with a smile.

Extend your understanding

A synonym is a word that has the same meaning, or nearly the same meaning, as another word. For example, **acute** and **developed** are synonyms. However, **acute** has a stronger meaning. In other words, **acute** means very, very developed.

 Complete the sentences by choosing the appropriate word or phrase. Use each word or phrase once. The words and phrases are synonyms, but the second word or phrase has a stronger meaning.

The first one is an example.

1. developed / acute

    Dogs have an **acute** sense of smell. It is 10,000 times stronger than a human's.
    Her ability to draw is **developed** for her age.

2. bad / inhospitable

    The climate is _____ . Nobody lives there.
    It was a _____ winter. It snowed until June.

3. sad / a tragedy

    Hundreds of people died in the fire. It was _____ .
    The ending to the movie was _____ . I wanted to cry.

4. tired / exhausted

    I don't know why I feel _____ today. I slept well.
    I'm _____ . I haven't slept all week.

5. negative / harsh

    Your words were _____ . He felt bad for months.
    You're never _____ . You always see the bright side of things.

Lesson 11

Environment

Global Warming

Pre-reading Activity

What do you KNOW about global warming?	What do you WANT to learn about global warming?	What did you LEARN about global warming?*

* Complete this column after you read the passage on the next page.

Vocabulary words

habitable	principal	accumulate
vast	emission	alleviate

Global Warming

The Earth is getting warmer, a trend commonly referred to as global warming. If global warming continues, it may have devastating results for future generations. The ice at the north and south poles will melt. Sea levels will rise. Low-lying coasts and islands will disappear under water. Places that usually get lots of rain will become hotter and drier. Hurricanes and tornadoes will increase in number. And fresh water will be in short supply.

What is causing global warming? Many different gases surround the Earth. Some of these gases are called greenhouse gases. The greenhouse gases trap the sun's heat. This natural process helps stabilize the Earth's temperature so that the planet remains **habitable**. If the greenhouse gases did not exist, much of the Earth would be frozen. However, these gases have been getting thicker and trapping more and more of the sun's heat. This increase in trapped heat is the cause of global warming.

Carbon dioxide (CO_2) is one of the **principal** greenhouse gases in the Earth's atmosphere. In nature, there is an exchange of carbon between the atmosphere, oceans and rivers, and all living things. For example, living trees absorb CO_2; dying and decaying trees release their stored CO_2 into the atmosphere. The Earth constantly recycles CO_2, which serves to balance the amount of CO_2 in the atmosphere.

> *Carbon dioxide is a gas made up of carbon and oxygen.*

Many scientists believe that human activities contribute to global warming. Burning fuels such as oil, gas, and coal increases greenhouse gases such as CO_2. We add to global warming whenever we heat the oven, burn oil or gas to heat our homes, or cook on the barbecue. The CO_2 that is produced by human activity throws off the CO_2 balance in the atmosphere. Over 70 percent of the extra CO_2 in the atmosphere comes from burning fuels. The Earth cannot absorb the extra CO_2 fast enough, so the CO_2 **accumulates**. The amount of carbon that we produce through our lifestyle choices is called a "carbon footprint."

The destruction of **vast** areas of the Earth's forests and jungles also contributes to global warming. Forests absorb and store approximately 10 percent of North America's CO_2 **emissions**. When forests are cut down, huge amounts of CO_2 are released back into the atmosphere. And fewer trees are left to absorb CO_2.

Governments can **alleviate** the effects of global warming by investing money in cleaner sources of power, such as wind and solar power. People can alleviate the effects of global warming by following the three Rs—reduce, recycle, and reuse.

Discussion

In what ways can people reduce their carbon footprint?

Check your understanding

 Circle the best meaning for each bolded word. Try to figure out what the word means by looking at the way it is used in the sentence.

1. Some places are more **habitable** than others. For example, the North Pole is too cold. Deserts are too hot. But Hawaii is just right.
   a. suitable to live in
   b. expensive to live in
   c. boring to live in

2. Smoking is a **principal** cause of lung cancer.
   a. not believable
   b. necessary
   c. main; most important

3. Your shopper's bonus points **accumulate** if you buy things regularly. You get 50 points for every $100 you spend.
   a. disappear completely
   b. increase gradually over time
   c. become less noticeable

4. The open sky is **vast**. It goes on forever and ever.
   a. hard to see
   b. limited
   c. huge

5. Factory **emissions** contribute a lot to pollution. But many factories are now producing goods in a way that cuts down on harmful emissions.
   a. something sent out or given off
   b. something that keeps an area clean
   c. something that people want to buy

6. The new bridge should **alleviate** the traffic problems.
   a. maintain; keep the same
   b. increase or cause to grow
   c. make easier to cope with

Boost your understanding

 Circle the answer that makes the most sense.

1. Which of the following would make a home less **habitable**?
   a. putting down a new carpet
   b. turning off the water supply
   c. painting the walls bright yellow

2. One **principal** concern that parents have about their kids is
   a. who their kids choose as friends.
   b. how their kids cut their hair.
   c. why their kids grow so fast.

3. The evidence against me started to **accumulate**. I was sure that I
   a. would fool the jury.
   b. was going to go to jail.
   c. did not commit the crime.

4. His knowledge of the insect world is **vast**. He
   a. talks about insects a lot.
   b. is a scientist who studies insects.
   c. is afraid of insects.

5. The **emissions** from the bus increased as the day went on. The bus
   a. had just had a tune-up.
   b. was burning too much oil.
   c. got a flat tire.

6. She **alleviated** the pain. She
   a. fell down the stairs.
   b. refused to visit a doctor.
   c. took a pill.

Apply your understanding

 Write an answer for each of the questions. Use complete sentences.

1. Name three basic things that make a place **habitable**.

   _____
   _____

2. The tasks a person has to complete might start to **accumulate** if a person is sick. What else might cause daily tasks to build up?

   _____
   _____

3. There is a lot of tension between your partner and your best friend. What is one way to **alleviate** the tension?

   _____
   _____

Complete the sentences with your own ideas.

4. My **principal** pet peeve is _____
   _____.

5. Nobody lives in the area because of the **emissions** from the factory. The emissions _____.

6. I looked out across the **vast** _____ and saw nothing but open blue water.

Apply your understanding

D Write sentences using the vocabulary words.

habitable _____

_____

accumulate _____

_____

alleviate _____

_____

principal _____

_____

emission _____

_____

vast _____

_____

"not see the forest for the trees"

idiom for today

She "didn't see the forest for the trees." She spent so much time checking spelling and punctuation during the exam that she didn't have time to finish the essay.

"Not seeing the forest for the trees" means not being able to see the big picture because of focusing too much attention on details.

Extend your understanding

 In each set of sentences, underline the meaning for the bolded word.

The first one is an example.

1. All she wanted was a **habitable** apartment.
   Some apartments were so rundown that they were not <u>fit to live in</u>.

2. The **principal** reason for cancelling the game was the bad weather.
   Lack of interest in playing was another main reason.

3. She has a **vast** knowledge of Canadian history.
   The amount of knowledge she has seems limitless.

4. I'll cut down on the hours I work every week to **alleviate** stress.
   This will make it easier to cope with small problems.

5. The garbage **accumulated** in the streets during the garbage strike.
   As the hills of garbage slowly increased, people complained more.

Lesson 12

Popular Culture

Extreme Sports

Pre-reading Activity

What do you KNOW about extreme sports?	What do you WANT to learn about extreme sports?	What did you LEARN about extreme sports?*

* Complete this column after you read the passage on the next page.

Vocabulary words

bizarre	extreme	enhance
alternative	timid	scorn

Extreme Sports

Climbing to the top of a high-rise building and then jumping off with a parachute may seem like a **bizarre** way to have fun. From this height, it is a quick fall to earth with no room for mistakes. If the parachute does not open, there is no time to open a reserve chute. Little wonder that this sport has a high fatality rate. Yet, BASE jumping is a popular sport among skydivers who want something even more thrilling than jumping out of a plane.

BASE jumping, car racing, mountain climbing, bungee jumping, and skydiving are all **extreme** sports. Each extreme sport has its own subculture. The members of the subculture often dress in a unique way and use *jargon*.

> *Jargon* is special language or vocabulary that is used by a specific group of people. For example, nurses use medical jargon.

Extreme sports push people to the limits of their physical abilities—and the risks are high. These sports attract thousands of people even though they are dangerous. Not surprisingly, most people who do extreme sports are young adults. Why do people choose to flirt with death?

One answer may lie in the way thrill-seekers' brains work. Research suggests that thrill-seekers' brains have special receptors that absorb a chemical called dopamine. Dopamine acts like a drug and **enhances** a person's mood. Thrill-seekers pursue high-risk activities that increase the production of dopamine. Not all people with this brain chemistry jump off buildings with a parachute, however. People who like to take risks find **alternative** ways to meet their need for excitement. They might gamble or choose dangerous jobs such as fighting wildfires.

People also choose extreme sports because they like being part of a special group. Most people avoid extreme sports, so the few who get involved belong to an exclusive club. The members of the extreme sports club feel unique because they have the courage to risk their lives. Club members enjoy the friendship of other thrill-seekers and the respect of people who are too **timid** to do extreme sports. Perhaps as important, being in the extreme sports club separates young risk takers from older adults, who may look at these sports with **scorn**.

Extreme sports offer young adults thrills and adventure at a time when they are finding out who they are and what they believe in. Because of this, extreme sports continue to be popular, despite the danger.

Discussion

Why do you think some young people like to participate in extreme sports?

Check your understanding

 Circle the best meaning for each bolded word. Try to figure out what the word means by looking at the way it is used in the sentence.

1. Wearing sunglasses indoors at night is a **bizarre** thing to do.
   a. strange
   b. ordinary
   c. good

2. Jasmine suffered from **extreme** pain when her tooth was pulled.
   a. too much
   b. too little
   c. just right

3. People try to **enhance** their chances of getting a job in many ways. For example, they take courses and update their resumes.
   a. improve
   b. limit
   c. ruin

4. Franco believes in **alternative** health care. He stays healthy by using herbs rather than prescription drugs.
   a. expensive or time-consuming
   b. not usual or traditional
   c. unlucky or illegal

5. Bullies usually pick on **timid** kids who are afraid to fight back.
   a. smart
   b. big
   c. shy

6. She looked with **scorn** at anyone who did sports. She felt sports were a waste of time and money.
   a. admiration with some jealousy
   b. strong dislike and disrespect
   c. feelings of regret and sadness

Boost your understanding

 Circle the answer that makes the most sense.

1. It would be okay to wear a **bizarre** outfit to
   a. a funeral.
   b. work.
   c. a funky night club.

2. His reaction to seeing the spider was **extreme**. He
   a. looked closely at the spider.
   b. ignored the spider.
   c. fainted.

3. What would **enhance** the taste of a meal?
   a. using a knife and fork
   b. adding spices
   c. freezing the food

4. She found an **alternative** way to cook fish.
   a. She fried the fish in a pan.
   b. She baked the fish in the oven.
   c. She wrapped the fish in foil and put it in the dishwasher.

5. An angry woman started to yell at a **timid** man on the bus. The man
   a. started to laugh at the woman.
   b. yelled back at the woman.
   c. looked quietly down at the floor of the bus.

6. I felt nothing but **scorn** for his behaviour at lunch because he
   a. insulted the server over and over again.
   b. ate a lot.
   c. did not finish his meal.

Apply your understanding

 Write an answer for each of the questions. Use complete sentences.

1. If someone insults you, you can insult them back. What is an **alternative** way of handling this situation?

   _____
   _____

2. What is the most **bizarre** thing you have ever seen or heard?

   _____
   _____

3. How can people **enhance** their memory?

   _____
   _____

Complete the sentences with your own ideas.

4. She went to the plastic surgeon for an **extreme** makeover. After the makeover, she

   _____.

5. I feel nothing but **scorn** at the way she treats animals. She _____

   _____.

6. My friend was too **timid** to _____,

   so I helped her by _____.

Apply your understanding

 **D** Write sentences using the vocabulary words.

alternative _____

_____

bizarre _____

_____

enhance _____

_____

extreme _____

_____

scorn _____

_____

timid _____

_____

"risk life and limb"

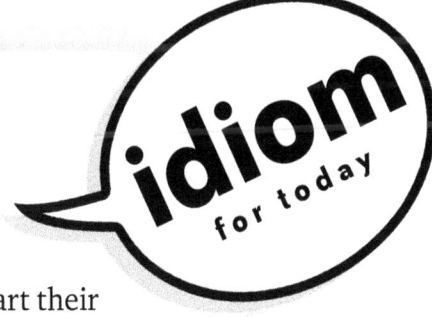

Auto racers "risk life and limb" every time they start their engines.

"Risking life and limb" means doing something so dangerous that it could cause serious injury or death.

Extend your understanding

The word **alternative** is used to describe something that is outside, or different from, what we usually see in our society. For example, parents who home-school their children believe in **alternative** education.

 Look at the following lists of items. Circle one (or more) **alternative** items in each list. Explain your choices.

Family Life	Health Care	Music
gay marriage	hypnosis	punk rock
common-law marriage	massage	new age
single-parent family	drugs	folk music
living in a commune	acupuncture	gospel
marriage of one man and one woman	Chinese medicine	classical

Wordsearch 3

L	X	Y	R	X	V	I	G	I	L	A	N	T	B	O	E	U	K
Q	J	W	N	M	L	T	I	M	I	D	Q	A	E	K	J	L	Q
O	P	U	A	Q	U	O	X	Q	J	I	M	A	G	E	K	R	F
Y	A	Q	D	E	X	T	R	E	M	E	I	Z	S	K	N	E	S
U	P	E	R	P	E	N	A	R	V	K	T	X	H	U	Z	M	P
X	A	M	E	M	S	K	S	B	I	Z	A	R	R	E	I	I	E
E	T	I	N	A	L	L	E	V	I	A	T	E	W	T	N	S	C
N	H	P	A	N	Z	H	A	C	T	E	M	D	S	P	H	S	I
H	Y	L	L	W	G	B	V	B	X	Y	T	A	U	D	O	I	E
A	S	V	I	C	I	N	I	T	Y	T	V	P	Q	I	S	O	S
N	K	B	N	L	A	N	S	Q	C	G	D	D	P	P	P	N	K
C	C	Q	E	A	L	T	E	R	N	A	T	I	V	E	I	S	C
E	W	A	C	C	U	M	U	L	A	T	E	C	R	C	T	Q	M
R	F	G	M	T	R	A	C	E	P	Q	D	D	Q	I	A	X	V
Y	O	Q	S	L	C	A	U	T	I	O	U	S	L	Y	B	Q	J
C	C	U	P	R	I	N	C	I	P	A	L	L	R	Q	L	N	A
S	C	R	U	T	I	N	I	Z	E	J	Z	A	F	X	E	P	L
I	Z	F	S	O	H	S	U	B	H	Y	L	R	V	J	E	G	F

scrutinize   vigilant   cautiously   trace   adrenaline   image
apathy   vicinity   principal   accumulate   vast   emissions
bizarre   extreme   enhance   alternative   timid   species
inhospitable   alleviate

Lesson 13

Health

Alzheimer's Disease

Pre-reading Activity

What do you KNOW about Alzheimer's disease?	What do you WANT to learn about Alzheimer's disease?	What did you LEARN about Alzheimer's disease?*

* Complete this column after you read the passage on the next page.

Vocabulary words

autopsy   abnormal   widespread
debilitating   radical   passive

Alzheimer's Disease

A 51-year-old female suffered memory loss and had difficulty expressing her thoughts. She also had problems understanding what people said to her. For five years, the woman's symptoms worsened and eventually, she could not leave her bed. After the woman's death, her doctor performed an **autopsy**. He found that the area of the brain responsible for thinking, memory, speech, and reasoning had shrunk. The brain showed **abnormal** fatty deposits and many dead and dying brain cells. The year was 1906. The doctor's name was Dr. Alois Alzheimer.

The condition the doctor discovered now bears his name—Alzheimer's disease. The disease is **widespread**. Nearly 400,000 Canadians and 4,500,000 Americans suffer from this **debilitating** disease. These numbers will increase as populations age. Currently, there is no cure for Alzheimer's.

Alzheimer's disease can strike people as young as 30. Symptoms range from forgetfulness to changes in behaviour to **radical** mood swings. For example, Alzheimer victims can be easygoing and happy one moment, angry the next. They may begin to imagine events, like a loved one stealing or their partner having an affair. As well, daily tasks can become confusing. On a hot summer day, a person with Alzheimer's might put on winter boots and gloves. Or they might put popsicles in the oven and try to bake bread in the fridge.

Some people with Alzheimer's become **passive**. They sit in front of the television for hours. A once early riser will sleep until noon every day. Another who used to love to exercise will want to remain at rest.

Easy routine tasks become difficult because of memory loss. People with Alzheimer's can get lost in their own neighbourhoods. They have no idea where they are or how to find their way home. Their vocabulary becomes more limited because they forget simple words. A person with Alzheimer's might describe a cooking pot as "that thing you use to heat up food."

With no cure, it might seem the onset of Alzheimer's brings hopelessness. But with proper care, people with Alzheimer's can maintain the quality of their lives for many years. Drugs are available that slow the progress of the disease. Quiet, calm environments reduce the possibility of patients becoming confused. Routine, appropriate exercise, and gentle music all help.

Caregivers can further reduce potential moments of confusion by speaking clearly and directly. For example, "Do you want to eat breakfast now?" is easier to respond to than "Do you want to eat breakfast or take a bath?" Finally, being aware of the patient's personal comfort at all times is important.

No magic formula exists to prevent Alzheimer's disease. However, staying healthy and active both physically and mentally as one ages can reduce the risk of getting Alzheimer's.

Discussion

What can people do to remain both physically and mentally active as they age?

Check your understanding

 Circle the best meaning for each bolded word. Try to figure out what the word means by looking at the way it is used in the sentence.

1. The **autopsy** was unclear. The victim may have died from drowning or fluid on the lungs.
   a. report that describes a patient's lifestyle
   b. examination of a dead body to find out the cause of death
   c. study that shows how people react to different situations

2. The results of the blood test were **abnormal**. The doctor was concerned. She asked for more tests to be done.
   a. right or correct
   b. better than normal
   c. different from the usual in a negative way

3. People all over the country listened to the Prime Minister's speech. There was **widespread** interest in what he had to say.
   a. none or little
   b. limited or contained to a local area
   c. common over a huge area or among many people

4. His lifestyle was **debilitating** to his health. He smoked, drank, stayed out all night, and lived on junk food.
   a. having no effect on; not important
   b. making something less strong or healthy
   c. adding life or colour to something

5. The barking dog was driving me crazy! I took **radical** action—and shot it.
   a. very new or different from what is usual or traditional
   b. careful; paying almost too much attention to detail
   c. hidden from sight; unknown

6. The workers' **passive** reaction to the boss' crazy rules is not a good sign. The workers need to speak their minds.
   a. not active; allowing things to happen without trying to make changes
   b. angry; arguing with strong words to make a point
   c. surprising or unusual

Boost your understanding

 Circle the answer that makes the most sense.

1. She spent days carrying out an important **autopsy**. Her work
   a. included interviewing the victim.
   b. told the police that the victim had been murdered.
   c. gave the victim hope.

2. The doctor's behaviour was **abnormal**. He
   a. offered me a cigarette in his office.
   b. weighed me and checked my blood pressure.
   c. did not take any phone calls during my visit.

3. The use of cell phones is **widespread**.
   a. I have a cell phone.
   b. I know some people who have cell phones.
   c. I read that people in small African villages use cell phones.

4. The last 20 years has been **debilitating** to the country's economy. The country has
   a. developed new products to sell to other countries.
   b. been at war.
   c. improved its transportation system.

5. My ideas about education are **radical**. I believe
   a. we should replace all teachers with scientists.
   b. teachers should be paid more.
   c. students should take more field trips.

6. The population is **passive**. A lot of people do not
   a. vote.
   b. eat well.
   c. go to school.

Apply your understanding

C Write an answer for each of the questions. Use complete sentences.

1. The use of illegal drugs is **widespread**. Who do you think should be most responsible for reducing the use of illegal drugs? The government? Teachers and religious leaders? Individuals? Give a reason for your opinion.

   _____
   _____

2. A **passive** person would probably avoid arguments. Describe two other behaviours that you would see in a passive person.

   _____
   _____

3. What may seem **abnormal** to one person may seem normal to another person. How do people get their ideas about what is or is not normal?

   _____
   _____

Complete the sentences with your own ideas.

4. The **autopsy** showed that the victim_____
   _____.

5. After the third time my home was broken into, I took **radical** action. I _____
   _____.

6. Even though my neighbour has a **debilitating** disease, he still _____
   _____.

Apply your understanding

 **D** Write sentences using the vocabulary words.

widespread _____

_____

passive _____

_____

abnormal _____

_____

autopsy _____

_____

radical _____

_____

debilitating _____

_____

"jog someone's memory"

I tried to "jog his memory" by showing him pictures of the trip. But it was no use. He was only three years old when we took that trip.

"Jogging a person's memory" means saying or doing something that will help a person remember something.

Extend your understanding

 In each set of sentences, underline the meaning for the bolded word.

The first one is an example.

1. I was afraid that my kid was acting a bit **abnormal**.
   Then I realized teenagers aren't sane. They're just <u>weird</u>.

2. Body piercing is becoming more **widespread** in North America.
   Although it is risky, piercing is quite common among people everywhere.

3. That virus is **debilitating**. It attacks the digestive system.
   As the virus grows stronger, it makes the digestive system weaker.

4. I've made some **radical** changes in my lifestyle.
   Dad thinks the changes are great! But then he's not traditional either.

5. His **passive** behaviour in class is confusing.
   It's hard to tell if he understands or not. He goes along with everything.

6. I don't think I could watch an **autopsy**.
   I'm not a doctor. So the idea of examining the inside of a dead body makes me shiver.

Lesson 14

Wildlife

An Australian Pest

Pre-reading Activity

What do you KNOW about wild rabbits?	What do you WANT to learn about wild rabbits?	What did you LEARN about wild rabbits?*

* Complete this column after you read the passage on the next page.

Vocabulary words

livestock	ecosystem	indigenous
erosion	immunity	lethal

An Australian Pest

What animal is the biggest threat to the people of Australia? Some people might guess poisonous snakes and spiders. Few people would think of cute, harmless rabbits. While rabbits may be cute, the damage they do in Australia makes them far from harmless. Farmers lose millions of dollars each year because of rabbits. Rabbits eat crops, herbs, and grasses that are needed to feed **livestock**. Even worse, rabbits have a devastating effect on the environment.

In 1859, an English immigrant named Thomas Austin released 24 rabbits into the wild for hunting purposes. Because rabbits had no natural predators in Australia, rabbits spread quickly across the country. A single pair of rabbits can produce up to 30 young a year. By the 1920s, 24 rabbits had become 10 billion rabbits inhabiting every part of Australia.

The diet and habits of wild rabbits have changed Australia's **ecosystem**. The rabbits eat plants, trees, shrubs, grasses, roots, and seeds. Many **indigenous** types of vegetation are now extinct. The rabbits also cause soil **erosion** by eating the vegetation, digging for roots, and building *warrens*. The exposed topsoil, which contains nutrients, is blown or washed away. New plants do not grow well in the remaining soil because of the lack of nutrients. As well, rabbits compete with other wildlife for food. As a result, many small indigenous animals have become extinct.

> A *warren* is a system of underground tunnels that rabbits live in.

Australians have tried a variety of methods to control the rabbit population. In the early 1900s, a fence was built across western Australia to stop rabbits from spreading. The idea failed. Rabbits had already spread into the fenced area. Until the 1950s, farmers used traditional methods to kill rabbits. They trapped, shot, and poisoned rabbits. Farmers also destroyed rabbit warrens. These methods of killing rabbits had some success on a local level. But only for a short time.

In 1957, scientists used fleas to spread a virus among wild rabbits. At first, the virus caused a fatal illness in the rabbits. Over 90 percent of the wild rabbits died. But some rabbits developed an **immunity** to the virus. The rabbit population began to increase again. In 1996, scientists developed a new virus. But it has not worked as well as the first virus.

Scientists still believe injecting rabbits with a virus is the best method of control. Scientists are now working on a virus that will block female rabbits from getting pregnant. Using a virus to reduce the numbers of rabbits will decrease the need for more **lethal** controls like poisoning. After all, who wants to hurt cute, little bunnies?

Discussion

What can we learn about ecosystems from Australia's experience with rabbits?

Check your understanding

 Circle the best meaning for each bolded word. Try to figure out what the word means by looking at the way it is used in the sentence.

1. **Livestock**, such as cattle and sheep, need a lot of grazing land. Some people argue that raising livestock is bad for the environment.
   a. farm animals
   b. dead animals
   c. wild animals

2. In a forest **ecosystem**, the trees depend on the sun, rain, and soil to grow. Forest animals use the trees for food and shelter.
   a. camp, usually used by hunters
   b. stream or creek that runs through a wooded area
   c. the connection among all things that exist in a specific place

3. He grows **indigenous** plants as well as plants that come from different countries.
   a. coming from a different place
   b. living or existing in a place naturally
   c. growing quickly and without too much water

4. Over millions of years, mountains become hills because of **erosion** caused by wind, rain, ice, and snow.
   a. an organized buildup
   b. a quick blast
   c. a slow and gradual wearing away

5. Some babies get vaccinations to give them **immunity** to childhood diseases. For example, I never got the mumps as a child.
   a. safety from something
   b. ability to get something quickly
   c. information about something

6. Taking too much medicine can be **lethal**.
   a. good for you
   b. causing death
   c. cheap

Boost your understanding

B Circle the answer that makes the most sense.

1. The farmer's **livestock** was expensive to feed.
   a. The farmer was a vegetarian.
   b. The farmer owned a huge herd of cattle.
   c. The farmer's primary crop was coffee beans.

2. This **ecosystem** includes snakes, lizards, and scorpions. The ecosystem is in
   a. the Arctic.
   b. a desert.
   c. the bottom of the sea.

3. Many kinds of maple trees are **indigenous** to Canada. Maple trees
   a. have always been in Canada.
   b. were brought to Canada by Europeans.
   c. probably grow well in hot climates.

4. The riverbank was affected by **erosion**. The river was getting
   a. wider.
   b. narrower.
   c. deeper.

5. I have a natural **immunity** to colds and sore throats. I
   a. am quite healthy.
   b. recover from colds and sore throats quickly.
   c. always get colds and sore throats.

6. A **lethal** bolt of lightning struck the soccer player. She
   a. died.
   b. was badly hurt.
   c. went on to score the winning goal.

Apply your understanding

 Write an answer for each of the questions. Use complete sentences.

1. Do you think people who own a **lethal** weapon, such as a gun, should be required to obtain a licence?

   _____

   _____

2. Some people do not eat meat because a lot of land is needed to support **livestock** such as cattle. Do you think people should stop eating meat in order to free up land to grow food? Give a reason for your opinion.

   _____

   _____

3. Some people get **immunity** from the law. For example, a gang member may not go to jail for his crimes if he gives the police information. Do you think that giving people immunity from the law is a good idea? Give a reason for your opinion.

   _____

   _____

Complete the sentences with your own ideas.

4. _____ and _____ are important parts of a pond's **ecosystem**.

   _____.

5. The city planned to slow the riverbank's **erosion** by _____

   _____.

6. He decided to plant **indigenous** shrubs in his flower garden because _____

   _____.

Apply your understanding

 Write sentences using the vocabulary words.

lethal _____

_____

livestock _____

_____

immunity _____

_____

ecosystem _____

_____

erosion _____

_____

indigenous _____

_____

"dust bunnies"

The room looks clean, but I saw "dust bunnies" under the couch.

"Dust bunnies" are balls of dust that form in places that are not swept or dusted often.

Extend your understanding

Names affect how people see themselves and how they are seen by others. Names can become negative and take power away from a group of people. **First Nations** people used to be called **Indians**. The name **Indian** was a name given to **First Nations** people by Europeans. Groups of people change their name to show society a truer identity of their group.

A name, such as smokers, volunteers, and criminals, can show a common characteristic or behaviour among a group of people. Or, a name such as Quebecois or Albertan, can show where people come from. If a group of people were born in the region they live in, they are named **indigenous** people.

 Look at the pairs of names.
Which name is more positive? Explain your choice.

unemployed people

people who are between jobs

immigrants

new Canadians

Inuit

Eskimo

homemaker

housewife

old people

senior citizens

boss

employer

Lesson 15

Environment

The Sydney Tar Ponds

Pre-reading Activity

What do you KNOW about the Sydney tar ponds?	What do you WANT to learn about the Sydney tar ponds?	What did you LEARN about the Sydney tar ponds?*

*Complete this column after you read the passage on the next page.

Vocabulary words

hazardous   contaminated   sludge
defect   controversy   reclaimed

The Sydney Tar Ponds

Cape Breton, Nova Scotia, is famous for its natural beauty: towering cliffs, sandy beaches, and scenic waterfalls. But Sydney—the largest urban centre on Cape Breton Island—is well-known for a very different reason. One of the largest **hazardous** waste sites in Canada was located in the heart of Sydney. The local people called this waste site the Tar Ponds.

When Sydney's steel mill opened in 1901, it was a source of wealth and employment for the city. By 1912, the mill was producing close to half of Canada's steel. Fifty years later, the steel mill experienced financial difficulties. Consequently, little money was spent to reduce pollution. The steel mill finally closed in 2001. The mill left an awful mess for the city and the people who live there—almost 250 acres of contaminated land. The **contaminated** land includes the old steel mill, a dump, the coke ovens, and a stream.

The coke ovens produced toxic waste, which was carried away by the stream. The stream emptied into an *estuary* that flowed into Sydney Harbour. This toxic waste filled the estuary with a variety of coal-based contaminants and **sludge**. This area—the size of three city blocks—formed the Tar Ponds.

> An *estuary* is an area where a river or stream empties into the sea.

The Tar Ponds contained cancer-causing chemicals. People living near the site complained of headaches, nosebleeds, and breathing problems. Sydney had one of the highest rates of cancer, birth **defects**, and miscarriages in Canada.

In the 1980s, residents began to demand that the site be cleaned up. At that time, the mill was still open. People could not agree on the best way of cleaning up the pollution. Some people wanted to dig up and destroy every bit of contamination. Others felt that digging up the contaminated area would cause more damage. The **controversy** over the cleanup plan lasted for 22 years. Finally in 2004, the governments of Canada and Nova Scotia set up a plan for cleaning up the site.

Almost ten years and $400 million later, the government officially opened Open Hearth Park, which sits on the **reclaimed** land of the Sydney tar ponds. Some people are not convinced that the reclaimed land is safe. The hazardous waste from the tar ponds is buried only two metres below the park, covered with layers of concrete mixed with sludge. Will this cleanup solution protect residents from being affected by the hazardous waste, and for how long? Only time will tell.

Discussion

Who should be responsible for cleaning up contaminated sites? Give reasons for your opinions.

Check your understanding

 Circle the best meaning for each bolded word. Try to figure out what the word means by looking at the way it is used in the sentence.

1. Working on a commercial fishing boat in the North is a **hazardous** job. There is always the chance of falling overboard and freezing in the icy waters.
   a. smelly
   b. difficult
   c. dangerous

2. The oil tanker spilled thousands of litres of oil into the sea. The **contaminated** waters caused the death of hundreds of seals.
   a. salty
   b. dirty
   c. cold

3. The flood left **sludge** in the houses along the riverbank. It took days for people to shovel themselves out of the heavy, gooey mess.
   a. a thick muddy substance
   b. broken bits of trees
   c. a fine dust

4. If a new TV has **defects**, it should be returned to the store.
   a. things that make something less than perfect
   b. things that make something hard to understand
   c. things that make something look new

5. The **controversy** about a proposed cat bylaw continued for many weeks. People could not agree whether it was a good idea or not.
   a. a strong misunderstanding among many people
   b. a strong agreement among many people
   c. a strong argument among many people

6. After the dump was covered over with tons of gravel and clean soil, the **reclaimed** land became a park.
   a. useful again
   b. polluted
   c. difficult to find

Boost your understanding

 Circle the answer that makes the most sense.

1. Some cleaning materials are **hazardous** because they
   a. remove dirt.
   b. contain toxic chemicals.
   c. are sold in supermarkets.

2. **Contaminated** food is likely to make you
   a. ill.
   b. hungry.
   c. full.

3. They could not sell their home because it was too close to a pond full of **sludge**. The home was probably near
   a. an industrial site.
   b. an airport.
   c. a river valley.

4. The new toaster had a **defect**.
   a. The toaster was not cheap.
   b. The toast was always burned.
   c. The toast was ready in three minutes.

5. In a newspaper, letters about a **controversy** will probably express
   a. the same opinions.
   b. different opinions.
   c. silly opinions.

6. That park is built on **reclaimed** land. The land used to be
   a. under water.
   b. full of people.
   c. farmers' fields.

Apply your understanding

 Write an answer for each of the questions. Use complete sentences.

1. Some contaminated land is **reclaimed** for housing. Would you be willing to live on land that was once full of chemicals? Why or why not?

   _____
   _____

2. You buy a pair of jeans. You notice a **defect**. The zipper keeps getting stuck. Do you take the jeans back to the store? Why or why not?

   _____
   _____

3. Neighbours sometimes get in a **controversy** over community issues. Name one community issue that you would speak up for or against.

   _____
   _____

Complete the sentences with your own ideas.

4. Smoking is **hazardous** to your health because _____
   _____.

5. _____ the **contaminated** pool of water.

6. _____ because it was full of **sludge**.

Apply your understanding

D Write sentences using the vocabulary words.

reclaimed _____

_____

defect _____

_____

controversy _____

_____

hazardous _____

_____

contaminated _____

_____

sludge _____

_____

"waste your breath"

You're "wasting your breath" trying to explain computers to me. I'm not interested!

"Wasting your breath" means wasting your time talking.

Extend your understanding

Words can have different forms. For example,

contaminate is a verb (an action word)
contamination is a noun (a person, place, or thing)
contaminated is an adjective (a describing word)

 Circle the correct word form. The first one is an example.

1. (Contaminate / Contamination / **Contaminated**) waste should be stored according to rules and regulations.

2. Sea animals cannot live in (pollute / pollution / polluted) seas and oceans.

3. The people live near the (contaminate / contamination / contaminated) river. They are afraid the (contaminate / contamination / contaminated) will affect their health.

4. Don't (pollute / pollution / polluted)!

5. (Pollute / Pollution / Polluted) causes lung and heart disease.

6. Germs can (contaminate / contamination / contaminated) a wound if the wound is not cleaned properly.

Lesson 16

Popular Culture

Identity Theft

Pre-reading Activity

What do you KNOW about identity theft?	What do you WANT to learn about identity theft?	What did you LEARN about identity theft?*

* Complete this column after you read the passage on the next page.

Lesson 16

Vocabulary words

impersonate	fraud	forge
accountable	vital	diligent

Identity Theft

Identity theft is the fastest growing crime in North America. Identity thieves steal and use personal information such as names and addresses, social insurance numbers, and credit card numbers. Using someone's personal information without permission is identity theft. And it is a crime.

Identity thieves find personal information by stealing wallets and purses. Or they steal mail from mailboxes. Some identity thieves go through garbage bins to find documents that people have discarded. Others will even pretend to be landlords, employers, or creditors in order to get personal information. Once identity thieves have personal information, they can **impersonate** the victim. Identity thieves can open up a bank account and take out a loan under the victim's name. Or they can open up a credit card account and go on a shopping spree. This type of **fraud** can be extremely profitable for identity thieves.

Identity thieves use personal information to commit other crimes as well. For instance, they can use a stolen name and computer password to buy child porn on the Internet. Or identity thieves may **forge** documents such as car licences and passports.

Victims of identity theft quickly see that dealing with identity theft can be much harder to deal with than replacing stolen property. Tracing identity thieves is often impossible. The victims may be held **accountable** for the thieves' debts and their crimes. Victims then need to prove their innocence. Over the course of months or years, victims may spend hours and hours gathering information and contacting creditors. In the meantime, victims may face other problems such as not being able to borrow money or get insurance.

Rich or poor, anyone can fall victim to identity theft. Taking steps to protect personal information is **vital**. Find a safe place in your home to keep important documents such as birth certificates or social insurance cards. Never give out personal information to people you do not know. Never give out information to people who phone or email about special offers. Cut up documents like old cheques, bank statements, or income tax returns before throwing them away. Destroy old bank and credit cards. Do not let mail collect in your mailbox. Avoid using *PINs* that are easy to guess, like a birth date or part of a phone number. Change passwords frequently.

> ▶ *PIN* stands for Personal Identification Number. People need a PIN to use a bank card, for example.

The best way to prevent identity theft is to be **diligent** about protecting personal information. If you think you have been a victim of identity theft, report the crime right away.

Discussion

Do you think some people are more at risk of falling victim to identity theft than others? Explain your answer.

Check your understanding

 Circle the best meaning for each bolded word. Try to figure out what the word means by looking at the way it is used in the sentence.

1. Comedians sometimes **impersonate** famous people to make us laugh.
   a. take on the character of
   b. ignore the funny part of
   c. live with for a short time

2. Writing a cheque on another person's bank account is **fraud**. You can go to jail.
   a. a way to help someone
   b. a way to trick someone
   c. a way to borrow money

3. The young girl knew how to **forge** her mother's signature. So she always signed her report cards with her mother's name.
   a. make a copy of something to trick others
   b. write something so it is clear to read
   c. print in capital letters

4. Young drivers must be **accountable** for how they drive. That's why it is important to send them to driving school.
   a. nervous about
   b. not aware of
   c. responsible for

5. The bright rays of the sun can damage your eyes. Wearing sunglasses is **vital**.
   a. very important
   b. fashionable
   c. strange

6. The **diligent** employee received a raise after being with the company only three months.
   a. careful and steady
   b. always late
   c. easy to get along with

Boost your understanding

 Circle the answer that makes the most sense.

1. Criminals have been known to **impersonate** police officers in order to
   a. become more honest.
   b. join the police force.
   c. commit a crime.

2. People commit **fraud** because they want to
   a. steal something for themselves.
   b. help others find missing money.
   c. go to jail for a short period of time.

3. She was traveling with a passport that she **forged**. She
   a. applied to the government for the passport.
   b. travelled for a long time.
   c. was nervous whenever she crossed a border.

4. He is not **accountable** for his actions. He
   a. never admits when he makes a mistake.
   b. likes to do nice things for people.
   c. counts the times people make him angry.

5. It became **vital** for him to have his ears checked. He
   a. had not had his ears checked for over six months.
   b. could not hear the phone ringing anymore.
   c. could hear the sound of a pin drop.

6. He was **diligent** when it came to recording his expenses. He
   a. always ended up spending more money than he had.
   b. wrote down the cost of everything he bought.
   c. often made mistakes when adding up his expenses.

Apply your understanding

C Write an answer for each of the questions. Use complete sentences.

1. Have you or a friend ever been a victim of **fraud**? Describe what happened.
   _____
   _____

2. What **vital** signs does a doctor measure during a physical exam?
   _____
   _____

3. Some companies produce unhealthy food. Do you think that these companies should be **accountable** for the effects their products have on people?
   _____
   _____

Complete the sentences with your own ideas.

4. In order to **forge** a signature, you have to _____
   _____.

5. It's easy to **impersonate** my _____ because he/she _____
   _____.

6. I'm quite **diligent** when I _____.

Apply your understanding

 Write sentences using the vocabulary words.

fraud _____

_____

vital _____

_____

accountable _____

_____

forge _____

_____

impersonate _____

_____

diligent _____

_____

"thick as thieves"

Those two kids are as "thick as thieves." They do everything together.

Being "thick as thieves" means being very close and loyal friends.

Extend your understanding

A synonym is a word that has the same meaning, or nearly the same meaning, as another word. For example, **vital** and **important** are synonyms. However, the difference between the two is that **vital** has a stronger meaning. In other words, **vital** means very, very important.

 Complete the sentences by choosing the appropriate word or phrase. Use each word or phrase once. The words and phrases are synonyms, but the second word or phrase has a stronger meaning.

The first one is an example.

1. important / vital

   Breathing is **vital** to life.

   Having someone in your life to love is **important**.

2. angry / livid

   He was _____ because his son forgot his mother's birthday.

   He was _____ because his son wrecked the family car.

3. big / enormous

   His apartment is _____ for one person. A family of ten could live in it.

   His apartment is _____ for one person. It has two bathrooms.

4. sad / depressed

   I was so _____ the other day. I stayed in bed all day and cried.

   I was so _____ the other day. I felt better after going for a walk.

5. hot / scalding

   The water was _____ . It had just boiled.

   The water was _____ . It felt good on my skin.

6. scared / terrified

   She woke up to see a stranger in her bedroom. She was _____ .

   She woke to hear loud voices in the alley. She was _____ .

Word Search 4

Y	Z	G	D	C	S	H	K	Y	W	P	J	L	O	K	U	D	X
E	R	O	S	I	O	N	H	W	J	N	A	C	K	R	U	C	E
A	A	U	E	W	J	P	I	M	P	E	R	S	O	N	A	T	E
N	B	U	I	M	M	U	N	I	T	Y	Z	U	S	I	G	O	W
A	Z	N	T	W	K	Z	M	F	O	R	G	E	H	I	M	I	K
T	G	C	O	O	Y	M	V	V	R	F	C	N	J	H	V	J	P
L	C	V	V	R	P	N	K	R	E	C	O	S	Y	S	T	E	M
E	I	H	E	T	M	S	O	J	P	F	R	A	U	D	A	I	U
T	U	L	I	I	F	A	Y	X	G	B	I	W	F	B	C	C	N
H	X	J	L	A	G	K	L	A	T	K	D	E	K	R	C	P	S
A	C	O	N	T	A	M	I	N	A	T	E	D	X	A	O	Z	H
L	M	C	N	W	W	J	I	N	D	I	G	E	N	O	U	S	V
O	D	Z	R	U	W	I	D	E	S	P	R	E	A	D	N	Z	O
D	S	C	X	H	A	Z	A	R	D	O	U	S	Z	B	T	A	T
V	I	T	A	L	C	U	J	S	Z	R	A	D	I	C	A	L	B
N	Q	S	L	U	D	G	E	T	L	C	C	L	Q	O	B	F	H
U	U	C	O	N	T	R	O	V	E	R	S	Y	T	M	L	W	F
M	L	Y	O	Z	Y	W	D	E	F	E	C	T	S	B	E	R	K

autopsy	abnormal	widespread	radical	passive	ecosystem
erosion	indigenous	immunity	lethal	hazardous	contaminated
sludge	defects	controversy	impersonate	accountable	fraud
forge	vital				

Lesson 17

Health

Diabetes

Pre-reading Activity

What do you KNOW about diabetes?	What do you WANT to learn about diabetes?	What did you LEARN about diabetes?*

* Complete this column after you read the passage on the next page.

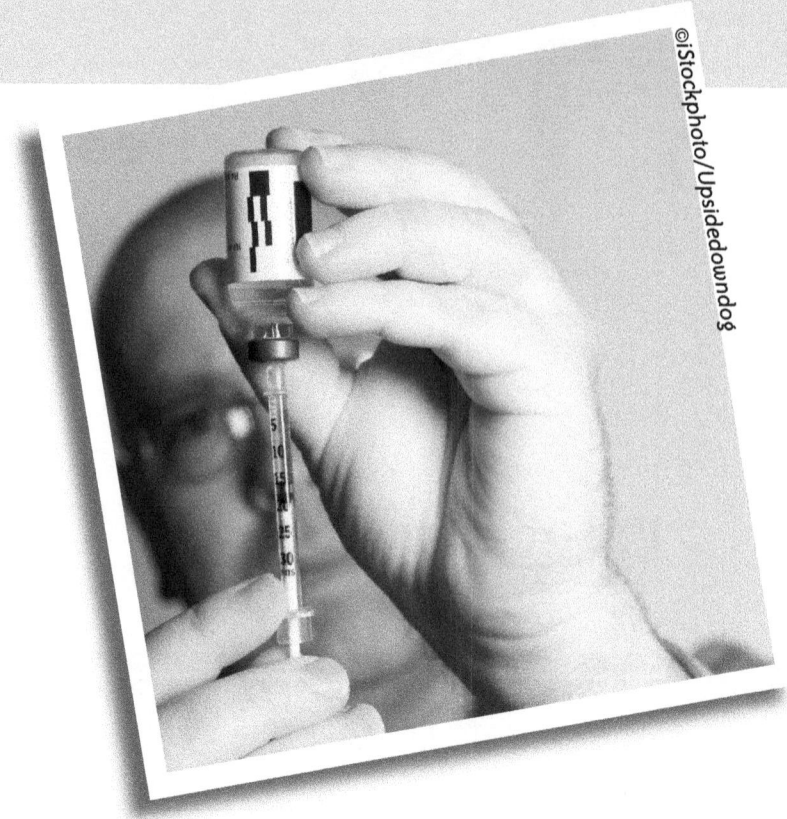

Vocabulary words

initiate	sufficient	convert
sedentary	obesity	monitor

Diabetes

Food fuels our bodies like gas fuels a car. Carbohydrates are an important source of fuel for our bodies. Our bodies change the carbohydrates we eat into a simple sugar called glucose. Glucose gives us energy. The amount of glucose in our blood normally goes up after we eat. This rise in glucose **initiates** the release of insulin. Insulin is a hormone that changes the glucose in our blood into energy.

Diabetes occurs when the body is unable to use the energy from food. This happens because the body does not properly use or produce **sufficient** amounts of insulin to **convert** glucose into energy. The buildup of glucose may cause many health problems such as eye, kidney, and nerve damage; poor blood circulation; and heart problems.

There are two main types of diabetes—type 1 and type 2. With type 1 diabetes, the body makes little or no insulin. With type 2 diabetes, a far more common form of diabetes, the body makes insulin but cannot use it properly. The most common symptoms of type 1 and type 2 diabetes are thirst, frequent urination, weight loss, and fatigue. With type 1 diabetes, the symptoms usually progress quickly and are often dramatic. With type 2 diabetes, the symptoms develop slowly and may go unnoticed for years.

Type 1 diabetes is usually diagnosed in children, teenagers, or young adults. People with type 1 diabetes often have a parent who has type 1 diabetes. In recent years, the number of children with type 2 diabetes has been increasing. Doctors believe that more children have type 2 diabetes because many children now lead **sedentary** lives. Children spend much of their free time sitting at computers or watching TV. Many children also eat high-fat snacks. Poor diet and lack of exercise cause children to gain weight, which puts children at risk for getting type 2 diabetes. Developing type 2 diabetes as an adult is also due in part to lack of exercise, poor diet, and **obesity**. But age becomes a contributing factor as well.

Having a knowledge of diabetes will help to prevent and control this disease. Type 1 diabetes is controlled with daily insulin injections and by **monitoring** glucose levels. People with type 1 diabetes learn to count carbohydrates and have a healthy, balanced diet. Type 2 diabetes can be not only controlled but also prevented by healthy eating, exercise, and weight loss. If necessary, people with type 2 diabetes can use medicine to help the body produce or use insulin more effectively.

Discussion

Which groups of people might be at risk for getting diabetes?

Check your understanding

 Circle the best meaning for each bolded word. Try to figure out what the word means by looking at the way it is used in the sentence.

1. He likes to **initiate** projects in his community. Last year, he started a community garden. This summer he wants to organize an art club for kids.
   a. talk about in an excited way
   b. start something going
   c. research carefully

2. He did not have **sufficient** savings in his account to buy a motorcycle. He bought a bicycle instead.
   a. enough to fill a need
   b. easy to use or get at
   c. coming from many places or sources

3. She started a small business from her home. She needed office space, so she **converted** a part of her bedroom into a home office.
   a. changed from one thing into another
   b. sold a part of something to make extra money
   c. cleaned up a space

4. Many young children suffer from **obesity** because they eat too much junk food and get too little exercise.
   a. being too friendly
   b. being too active
   c. being overweight

5. Driving a bus is a **sedentary** job. I wonder if a lot of bus drivers gain weight because they sit for such long periods of time.
   a. routine or repeating itself
   b. not physically active
   c. interesting

6. Biologists **monitor** the movement of elk through the national parks. They want to find out if elks are affected by the building of highways.
   a. guide something to a certain place
   b. keep track of something for a specific purpose
   c. ignore by not paying attention

Boost your understanding

 Circle the answer that makes the most sense.

1. He **initiated** change in the workplace by calling for a union. The workplace
   a. did not change.
   b. changed the union.
   c. began to change.

2. The student had **sufficient** reason to be absent from class.
   a. The student went to class.
   b. The teacher accepted the student's absence.
   c. The student was sometimes bored in class.

3. She **converted** to Buddhism. She
   a. did not believe in Buddhism.
   b. used to be Christian.
   c. was not religious.

4. **Obesity** has become an issue throughout North America. North Americans
   a. enjoy playing sports.
   b. should be proud of their health care systems.
   c. need buses with wider seats.

5. He is quite **sedentary**. He
   a. watches TV every night.
   b. works hard every day.
   c. is young at heart.

6. His phone calls are being **monitored**.
   a. He didn't pay his phone bill.
   b. His phone is broken.
   c. He is in the mafia.

Apply your understanding

C Write an answer for each of the questions. Use complete sentences.

1. Giving tests is a traditional way to **monitor** how well students are doing. What are some other ways to monitor student progress?

   _____
   _____

2. Some people are not happy with their lives, but they find it hard to **initiate** change. Why is it hard sometimes to make changes in life?

   _____
   _____

3. What are the dangers of being **sedentary**?

   _____
   _____

Complete the sentences with your own ideas.

4. **Obesity** is a serious issue because _____
   _____.

5. When the server saw his tip, he _____ . I guess the amount of the tip was more than **sufficient**.

6. We need a couch that **converts** into a bed because _____
   _____.

Apply your understanding

 **D** Write sentences using the vocabulary words.

monitor _____
_____

initiate _____
_____

sedentary _____
_____

obesity _____
_____

sufficient _____
_____

convert _____
_____

"a clean bill of health"

I was not surprised that the doctor gave me "a clean bill of health." I take good care of myself.

Having "a clean bill of health" means being free of medical problems.

Extend your understanding

The word **initiate** has many meanings, but the main meaning of **initiate** is connected with the idea of starting something.

> **initiate**
> a. start something going
> b. formally accept a new member into a group
> c. teach someone the basic rules or ideas of something
> d. a new member to a club; a beginner

 Match the meaning of **initiate** in each sentence below with the definitions of **initiate** above. Write the letter of the definition in the blank beside the sentence.

The first one is an example.

___a___ 1. Insults often **initiate** heated arguments.

_____ 2. My aunt **initiated** me into the wonders of the insect world.

_____ 3. The agreement was **initiated** by both sides.

_____ 4. Good instructors **initiate** students into subject areas by building on what students already know.

_____ 5. The **initiates** into the club were given the secret password.

_____ 6. The soccer team **initiated** new players by throwing them into the shower with their clothes on.

_____ 7. In their 25th year, the group honoured the women who **initiated** their organization.

_____ 8. The gang **initiated** him by giving him a tattoo.

Lesson 18

Wildlife

Greyhound Racing

Pre-reading Activity

What do you KNOW about greyhound racing?	What do you WANT to learn about greyhound racing?	What did you LEARN about greyhound racing?*

* Complete this column after you read the passage on the next page.

Vocabulary words

| surplus | inhumane | ventilated |
| burden | bleak | docile |

Greyhound Racing

Greyhound racing remains a popular sport in many countries. In North America, millions of people attend greyhound races because they enjoy cheap entertainment. Bred for speed, the greyhounds can race around a 500-metre track in 30 seconds. But the main attraction of the greyhound races is the chance to win money. Every year, people bet millions of dollars on greyhound races. And champion greyhounds win big prize money for their owners. Sadly, many people are unaware of the dark side of this sport.

Every year, the owners breed tens of thousands of greyhounds, more than they can place at racetracks. This over breeding is motivated by the desire to produce winning dogs. From the time they are born, greyhounds are judged for their racing ability. About 30 percent of the dogs have the potential to become racers. The **surplus** dogs are killed.

The dogs start racing between 16 to 20 months of age. The racetrack, which is a combination of straight lanes and tight corners, does not provide a safe racing environment. As the dogs race around the tight corners, they sometimes bump into each other and get knocked down. This results in sprains, fractures, and broken bones. When a greyhound is injured or begins to lose races, its days are numbered.

A dog's life is not much better off the track. The dogs suffer from **inhumane** living conditions, because the owners are more concerned about making a profit. Greyhounds are caged in pens or crates for 18 to 22 hours a day. Some owners feed the dogs raw meat that comes from dying, diseased, and disabled animals. Eating this meat exposes the dogs to deadly bacteria, which can result in illness or death. Greyhounds are also susceptible to cold and heat. Yet greyhounds often travel long distances in trucks that are not **ventilated** properly. The dogs arrive at the track suffering from heat exhaustion and dehydration.

Thousands of greyhounds are retired from racing every year at the age of four or five. Once their racing days are over, greyhounds become a financial **burden**. Most face a **bleak** future. Some owners sell greyhounds to universities for medical research. Other owners kill surplus dogs by extremely cruel methods such as drowning, shooting, or beating.

Throughout the world, greyhound racing faces growing opposition from animal rights organizations. A total of 34 states in the USA have banned the sport. Consequently, attendance at racetracks is dwindling, and revenue has significantly decreased.

Many non-profit organizations have been established to rescue retired greyhounds. The volunteers in these organizations are dedicated to finding loving homes for these **docile** and affectionate dogs.

Discussion

Do you think animals should be used to provide entertainment?

Why or why not?

Check your understanding

 Circle the best meaning for each bolded word. Try to figure out what the word means by looking at the way it is used in the sentence.

1. The farmer kept two dozen eggs for her family and sold the **surplus** eggs at the weekly farmer's market.
   a. extra to what is needed
   b. less than what is needed
   c. lots of any one item

2. Children are sometimes **inhumane** to animals. They tease or hurt animals for fun. We need to teach children to treat all living things with kindness.
   a. afraid of
   b. cruel to
   c. respectful of

3. The bathroom is not **ventilated**, so it always feels hot and damp.
   a. letting in fresh air
   b. creating fresh air
   c. blocking fresh air

4. Zakara is raising two children and has a full-time job. The extra **burden** of looking after her sick mother-in-law is almost too much for her.
   a. something that is a pleasure to do
   b. something that is hard to do or deal with
   c. something that causes illness

5. Without stable homes or jobs, refugees may face a **bleak** future.
   a. full of joy
   b. not hopeful
   c. surprising

6. Dogs are sometimes used in care centres to help depressed patients. Of course, the dogs need to be **docile**.
   a. easily fed
   b. easily hidden
   c. easily managed

Boost your understanding

 Circle the answer that makes the most sense.

1. If you have **surplus** tools in your home, you may
   a. need to buy more.
   b. try to sell them in a garage sale.
   c. not be able to find them.

2. Many people in the world work under **inhumane** conditions. These people
   a. should not complain about their job.
   b. work long hours for little money.
   c. work under safe conditions.

3. He carried the injured bird home in a **ventilated** box. The bird
   a. couldn't breathe.
   b. was afraid.
   c. poked its beak through the holes.

4. The retired couple said they did not want the **burden** of
   a. living in an apartment.
   b. managing an apartment building.
   c. paying a low rent.

5. The rent is low, but the apartment building is in a **bleak** area. The building is
   a. on a sunny beach.
   b. in a hilly, wooded area.
   c. in an industrial area.

6. The **docile** child answered by saying,
   a. "I hate you! Leave me alone!"
   b. "Okay."
   c. "I'm busy. I'll do it later."

Apply your understanding

 Write an answer for each of the questions. Use complete sentences.

1. If your city or town had a **surplus** of money, how would you like the funds to be used?

   _____
   _____

2. The Society for the Prevention of Cruelty to Animals (SPCA) protects animals from **inhumane** treatment, or cruelty. Should we care about protecting animal rights? Why or why not?

   _____
   _____

3. People who are **docile** tend to go along with things. People who are outspoken speak their minds. Describe a situation in which it would be good to be outspoken.

   _____
   _____

Complete the sentences with your own ideas.

4. _____ sometimes feels like a **burden**, especially when I'm tired.

5. _____ because the room wasn't **ventilated**. I was so glad to get out of there.

6. On grey, **bleak** days, I _____ .

Apply your understanding

D Write sentences using the vocabulary words.

surplus _____
_____

inhumane _____
_____

docile _____
_____

burden _____
_____

ventilated _____
_____

bleak _____
_____

"in the doghouse"

Samuel has been "in the doghouse" all week because he was expelled from school.

Being "in the doghouse" means people are upset with you because you did something wrong.

Extend your understanding

 In each set of sentences, underline the meaning for the bolded word.

The first one is an example.

1. We ended up with a **surplus** of books for the sale.
   People were so generous. They donated <u>more</u> books <u>than</u> we <u>needed</u>.

2. People can be **inhumane** not only to animals but also to one another.
   What makes some people so mean? Are they just angry at the world?

3. Spray paint in a **ventilated** area. Open all doors and windows.
   Letting in fresh air will clean the air of toxic paint fumes.

4. Single parents often carry a heavy financial **burden**.
   Making ends meet is a hard thing to cope with, especially at a young age.

5. His future felt **bleak**. Then he met the love of his life.
   Sadly, she said that their future together was not promising.

6. Lions and tigers in a circus may seem tame and **docile**.
   I imagine they are not easy to train—and quite unpredictable.

Lesson 19

Environment

Water

Pre-reading Activity

What do you KNOW about the water you drink?	What do you WANT to learn about the water you drink?	What did you LEARN about the water you drink?*

*Complete this column after you read the passage on the next page.

Vocabulary words

ailment reservoir seep
organism sound stringent

Water

For most North Americans, getting a drink of clean water is as simple as turning on a tap. But if clean drinking water gets contaminated, it can have tragic results. In 2000, in Walkerton, Ontario, 7 people died from drinking contaminated water. Another 27 people suffered from serious kidney **ailments**. And 2,300 people had stomach problems. The city's water supply had been contaminated by manure from a nearby farm. In 1993, a parasite in Milwaukee's water led to 100 deaths and made 400,000 people ill. Cases of contaminated water are rare.

However, such cases do occur when water treatment systems break down or when the quality of water is not monitored.

Our basic water supply comes from rain. Rain falls into lakes, rivers, streams, and **reservoirs**, where it becomes a source of surface water. Rain also **seeps** through the ground, forming underground pools, streams, and rivers. Some underground water systems lie 30 m (98.4 ft) below the ground and extend for kilometres. Groundwater provides about 97 percent of the world's total supply of drinking water.

But water is easily contaminated. Surface water from a lake or groundwater from a well might look clean, but that does not mean it is safe to drink. **Organisms** in the water can come from natural sources such as minerals and rotting leaves. Humans can make water unsafe to drink too. Many farmers use a lot of chemicals that eventually seep into our water supply. The bacteria from livestock's manure can contaminate groundwater if the waste seeps into nearby wells or groundwater. Old mines contain metals that can pollute groundwater. Dumps and landfills can release chemicals into the ground.

Some chemicals and organisms just make the water taste bad. Others are harmful, or even deadly. So both groundwater and surface water need to be treated before reaching our taps. Water treatment involves removing leaves, twigs, mud, and tiny bits of grit. Chlorine is added to kill bacteria. Viruses and parasites are also eliminated. The treated water is stored in huge water tanks, where it is tested a final time. The water is then ready for transport to homes through large underground pipes called water mains.

People need a safe supply of water. In most communities, water quality is maintained by a **sound** water-monitoring system and **stringent** controls. Despite these standards, water can get contaminated. Since 1999, the U.S. government requires community water systems to send annual reports to the public. These reports provide consumers with information about the quality of their drinking water. The information in the reports reaches about 273 million people across the U.S.

Discussion

Do you think that communities in Canada, like those in the U.S., should get annual reports about the quality of their water? Give reasons for your opinion.

Check your understanding

 Circle the best meaning for each bolded word. Try to figure out what the word means by looking at the way it is used in the sentence.

1. Older people tend to have more **ailments** than younger people. That is why it is a good idea to have an affordable health care system.
   a. temper tantrums
   b. illnesses
   c. worries about safety

2. Big cities need several **reservoirs** to supply water to their residents. These big bodies of water hold huge amounts of water.
   a. man-made lakes where water is stored
   b. dry areas filled with waste
   c. huge trucks with tanks

3. Snow that melts slowly **seeps** into the ground, especially if the ground is warm.
   a. freezes quickly over
   b. makes a deep hole in
   c. flows slowly through

4. **Organisms** eat away at a dead animal's body. This is nature's way of getting rid of the dead bodies of wild animals.
   a. huge rocks or stones
   b. people who hunt
   c. living animals

5. The attendance policy was **sound**. Both students and teachers followed it without complaint.
   a. sensible or practical
   b. causing lots of noise
   c. not popular

6. Some religions have **stringent** food rules. Some foods cannot be eaten, or even prepared, along with other foods.
   a. wrong or not important
   b. strict or serious
   c. changed from time to time

Boost your understanding

 Circle the answer that makes the most sense.

1. Two common **ailments** are
   a. headaches and insomnia.
   b. lack of money and lack of time.
   c. long hair and beards.

2. Which of these looks like a **reservoir**?
   a. a fast-flowing river
   b. a puddle
   c. a huge pool of water

3. The water would not **seep** through the soil. The soil was
   a. sandy and full of stones.
   b. ready for planting.
   c. packed hard.

4. Which of the following do **organisms** need to survive?
   a. gas, coal, and oil
   b. shelter
   c. air and water

5. His advice was **sound**. I
   a. laughed at it.
   b. followed it.
   c. did not understand it.

6. Her budget was **stringent**. She
   a. counted every penny.
   b. spent money on crazy things.
   c. had a really good job.

Apply your understanding

 Write an answer for each of the questions. Use complete sentences.

1. Some parents have **stringent** rules for their teens regarding curfews. Do you think curfews for teens are necessary? Give a reason for your opinion.

   _____
   _____

2. Where does your drinking water come from? For example, does it come from a **reservoir** or a well?

   _____
   _____

3. There are many different ways to treat a serious **ailment**. Most people prefer modern medicine. Some prefer natural treatments that use herbs. Others try alternative treatments such as hypnosis or acupuncture. What kind of treatment do you trust? Give a reason for your choice.

   _____
   _____

Complete the sentences with your own ideas.

4. Water was **seeping** under the bedroom door because _____
   _____.

5. You can't see them, but there are many **organisms** _____
   _____.

6. The new shelving unit wasn't very **sound**. The day after I installed it, _____
   _____.

Apply your understanding

D Write sentences using the vocabulary words.

stringent _____
_____

reservoir _____
_____

ailment _____
_____

seep _____
_____

organism _____
_____

sound _____
_____

"in hot water"

The kids were "in hot water" for breaking a car window while playing street hockey.

Being "in hot water" means being in trouble and likely to be punished in some way.

Extend your understanding

The word **sound** has many meanings.

sound
a. sensible and practical
b. a noise; something that can be heard
c. free from disease or injury
d. in good condition; undamaged; free from defects
e. complete

 Match the meaning of **sound** in each sentence below with the definitions of **sound** above. Write the letter of the definition in the blank beside the sentence.

The first one is an example.

__c__ 1. She got through military training safe and **sound**.

_____ 2. That's just the **sound** of the kettle boiling.

_____ 3. Her arguments were **sound**. The judge granted her custody of the children.

_____ 4. The tests showed that his heart was **sound**.

_____ 5. He had a **sound** understanding of my problem. He understood every detail.

_____ 6. The table is old, but **sound**. Go ahead and pile books on it.

_____ 7. Happiness is having a **sound** mind.

Lesson 20

Popular Culture

Body Piercing

Pre-reading Activity

What do you KNOW about body piercing?	What do you WANT to learn about body piercing?	What did you LEARN about body piercing?*

* Complete this column after you read the passage on the next page.

Vocabulary words

remains	aspect	transition
underground	seedy	mainstream

Body Piercing

Body piercing has a rich history that goes back thousands of years. The oldest piercing is on the **remains** of a 5,000-year-old male body. The ears are pierced. Like people today, ancient peoples used body piercing to express a sense of identity.

Civilizations and tribes have used body piercing in all **aspects** of culture. The *Aztecs* used body piercing in religious ceremonies. The Aztec priests pierced their tongues to draw blood. They passed a rough rope through the hole in the tongue to cause great pain. Drawing blood and experiencing pain honoured the gods. The priests altered their state of being, or went into a trance. Being in a trance helped the priests to communicate with the gods.

> The *Aztecs* were an ancient civilization in Mexico.

In many cultures, body piercing defines and celebrates both the **transition** from childhood to adulthood and the distinctions among men and women. Many Indian women, particularly Hindus, have their noses pierced around the age of 16. Nose piercing is one way Hindus honor Parvathi, the goddess of marriage.

Women in India also get piercings for medical reasons. One medical practice in India is based on the belief that parts of the human body are connected to each other. In Northern India, some people believe that the left nostril is connected to the reproductive organs. Indian women pierce their left nostril with a ring or stud in the hopes of having an easier childbirth.

Body piercing allows people to reinvent themselves—to rebel, to follow fashion, or to experiment with new identities. In the 1960s, North American youth started to use body piercing as a way to rebel against traditional values. Hippies learned about nose piercing during their travels through India, and brought the custom to North America. During the 70s, body piercing was popular in the gay culture of San Francisco. In the 80s, the punk movement adopted body piercing. Body piercing was still seen as an **underground** fad. It was something that was done in **seedy** little shops in back streets.

Body piercing in North America became more common in the mid 90s. Body piercings began to show up on models and music video stars. Today, body piercings are growing in number among people from all walks of life. Youth, actors, sports figures, and middle-class parents pierce their lips, noses, eyebrows, and navels.

Throughout history, the art of body piercing has been used as an expression of culture. But now, like tattooing, body piercing may be on its way to becoming just one more **mainstream** industry—just one more thing for people to buy.

Discussion

Why do you think that people get body piercings today?

Check your understanding

 Circle the best meaning for each bolded word. Try to figure out what the word means by looking at the way it is used in the sentence.

1. Different cultures treat the **remains** of the dead in different ways. For example, in India, it is common to burn the body.
    a. corpse; dead body
    b. personal belongings
    c. friends and family

2. People use computers in every **aspect** of their life. Computers are used in schools, at home, and at work.
    a. way to do something
    b. part of something
    c. end of something

3. The **transition** from junior high to high school is not always easy. The study load is heavier, and students need to be more responsible.
    a. change from one situation or condition to another
    b. long walk that involves many twists and turns
    c. vacation time that is full of surprises

4. Punk rock started as part of the **underground** music scene. But now punk rock is quite common.
    a. seen everywhere; known by most people
    b. separate or hidden from the main part of society
    c. under the earth; in a deep hole

5. They met in a **seedy** bar outside of town to plan the murder. They knew there was no chance of running into any of their hotshot lawyer friends.
    a. popular or trendy
    b. having lots of fruit and vegetables
    c. not respectable or decent

6. A lot of Hollywood movies are **mainstream**. The goal of making a movie in Hollywood is to attract the biggest audience possible.
    a. inexpensive; doing something as cheaply as possible
    b. suitable for young people only
    c. matching the attitudes and values of most people in society

Boost your understanding

 Circle the answer that makes the most sense.

1. The young child cried over the **remains** of her parrot. The parrot
   a. had eaten some bad seed.
   b. had a broken wing.
   c. had escaped and flown away.

2. There are many **aspects** to this problem. The problem
   a. will cost a lot of money to solve.
   b. has an easy solution.
   c. is complicated.

3. The government of the country is in **transition**.
   a. The country is peaceful.
   b. The country will have the same leaders.
   c. The country has just had an election.

4. They belong to an **underground** club. The club
   a. was set up just recently.
   b. advertises itself in all the newspapers.
   c. might be doing something illegal.

5. We stayed in a **seedy** hotel when we went to Las Vegas.
   a. The hotel room was dirty and rundown.
   b. The room service was great.
   c. I felt safe and secure.

6. His beliefs on marriage are not **mainstream**. He believes that
   a. people should remarry every two or three years.
   b. marriage is a commitment.
   c. friends and family should be part of the wedding day.

Apply your understanding

 Write an answer for each of the questions. Use complete sentences.

1. Eating good food is one **aspect** of leading a healthy lifestyle. What are two other aspects of leading a healthy lifestyle?

   _____

   _____

2. Some people keep the **remains**, or the ashes, of their loved ones in an urn. How do you feel about this practice? Why?

   _____

   _____

3. Life means going through a lot of **transitions**. For example, starting a new job requires making changes or adjustments in your life. What other life events require periods of transition?

   _____

   _____

Complete the sentences with your own ideas.

4. The **seediest** place I have ever seen was _____.

5. When I hear the word **underground**, I think of _____

   _____.

6. My beliefs on _____ are pretty **mainstream**.

   But my beliefs on _____ are not.

Popular Culture   *Vocabulary Boosters Workbook 3*

Apply your understanding

D Write sentences using the vocabulary words.

aspect _____

_____

remains _____

_____

transition _____

_____

seedy _____

_____

underground _____

_____

mainstream _____

_____

"another hole in the head"

I'm so busy these days! I need more work to do like I need "another hole in the head."

Needing something like "another hole in the head" means you do not need the thing at all.

Extend your understanding

Word meanings can be literal or figurative. A literal meaning is concrete or basic. A figurative meaning uses a basic meaning in an interesting way.

For example, the literal meaning of **underground** is under the ground. (The underground water system needs repair.) A figurative meaning of **underground** is secret and usually illegal. (Underground organizations can overthrow rulers.)

The literal and figurative meanings of the word **underground** are connected. If something is underground, it is hidden from view.

 Look at the bolded words or phrases in each of the following pairs of sentences.
What is the literal meaning? What is the figurative meaning? How are the literal and figurative meanings connected?

1. The lost hikers followed the **main stream** out of the woods.
   Most radio stations play **mainstream** music.

2. It's impossible to count the number of **stars** in the sky.
   Music video **stars** make lots of money.

3. Please tell me what's going on. I hate being **in the dark**.
   Some children are afraid of being alone **in the dark**.

4. The action figure has a **rubber neck** that stretches out.
   A lot of people **rubberneck** when they pass by an accident.

Word Search 5

S	U	R	P	L	U	S	T	U	S	F	B	S	E	E	D	Y	S
Q	I	N	I	T	I	A	T	E	C	T	X	L	D	U	G	B	I
S	E	D	E	N	T	A	R	Y	X	F	R	Z	E	E	W	D	K
Y	J	T	J	H	T	H	I	Q	J	L	S	I	S	A	U	Z	K
O	I	S	U	F	F	I	C	I	E	N	T	V	N	P	K	F	T
F	K	C	C	X	K	H	F	I	E	K	O	E	E	G	W	E	C
U	N	D	E	R	G	R	O	U	N	D	B	N	M	T	E	F	B
W	X	F	J	B	U	R	D	E	N	H	E	T	M	W	J	N	N
S	V	N	G	D	O	C	I	L	E	E	S	I	M	T	H	E	T
H	P	N	T	C	O	N	V	E	R	T	I	L	F	R	Z	O	N
Z	Z	H	F	Q	H	A	M	O	R	G	T	A	U	A	Y	N	E
X	I	W	S	G	T	G	T	H	C	O	Y	T	W	N	S	F	X
U	O	D	Y	S	C	I	T	X	S	S	Q	E	N	S	E	E	A
H	F	M	A	I	N	S	T	R	E	A	M	D	Q	I	E	N	S
S	K	W	D	O	A	N	K	H	S	D	G	J	E	T	P	F	P
P	P	R	M	P	F	Q	N	V	Z	Y	A	C	D	I	G	F	E
Y	U	Z	Q	A	I	L	M	E	N	T	B	C	Q	O	D	L	C
R	E	S	E	R	V	O	I	R	T	J	D	K	I	N	W	F	T

initiate	convert	sufficient	sedentary	obesity	monitor
docile	bleak	ventilated	burden	ailment	seep
reservoir	aspect	transition	underground	seedy	mainstream
surplus	stringent				

Glossary

This glossary provides only one main meaning for each word. This meaning reflects the way the word was used in the passage.

A
abnormal *adj.* not normal
accountable *adj.* responsible
accumulate *vb.* to increase gradually over time
acute *adj.* highly developed
adrenaline *n.* a substance that causes the heart to beat faster and gives a person more energy, produced by the body when a person feels strong emotion such as fear or anger
ailment *n.* a sickness
alleviate *vb.* to make easier to cope with
alternative *adj.* not usual or traditional
apathy *n.* a feeling of not having interest in or emotion about something
aspect *n.* part of something
autopsy *n.* examination of a dead body to find out the cause of death

B
bizarre *adj.* very strange or unusual
bleak *adj.* not hopeful or promising
burden *n.* something that is hard to do or deal with; a load

C
cautious *adj.* careful with the intention of avoiding danger or risk
chaos *n.* complete confusion
composition *n.* the combination of different parts to make a whole
conduct *vb.* to allow to pass through or move from one place to another
constrict *vb.* to squeeze; to make smaller or more narrow
contaminated *adj.* dirty or dangerous because something harmful was added
controversy *n.* a strong disagreement among many people
convert *vb.* to change from one thing into another
corrupt *adj.* without moral beliefs
crave *vb.* to have a strong wish or desire for
currency *n.* money

D
debilitating *adj.* making something less strong or healthy
deface *vb.* to ruin the surface of something, usually by writing on it
defect *n.* a problem that makes something less than perfect
dehydration *n.* loss of water
devastation *n.* almost complete destruction
diligent *adj.* careful and steady
docile *adj.* easily controlled, taught or led

E
ecosystem *n.* the connection among all things in a specific place
emission *n.* something that is sent out or given off
enhance *vb.* improve; make better
eradicate *vb.* to get rid of completely
erosion *n.* a slow and gradual wearing away
excessive *adj.* extreme; going beyond what is usual or proper
exposed *adj.* not protected; uncovered
extinguish *vb.* put out
extreme *adj.* too much; more than normal limits

F
fatal *adj.* causing death; deadly
forge *vb.* to copy or make a copy of something, usually to do something illegal
fraud *n.* a way to trick someone
fret *vb.* to worry or be concerned
frigid *adj.* extremely cold

G
gangrene *n.* the death of human tissue due to loss of blood
global *adj.* around the world; worldwide

H
habitable *adj.* suitable to live in
hazardous *adj.* dangerous

I

ideal *adj.* exactly right
image *n.* a mental picture
immerse *vb.* to put something into a liquid so all parts are covered
immunity *n.* safety from the danger of getting a disease
impersonate *vb.* to take on or copy the character of someone
impression *n.* the effect something has on someone's feelings or thoughts
indigenous *adj.* native; produced, living or existing naturally in a place
inhospitable *adj.* hard to survive in
inhumane *adj.* cruel
initiate *vb.* to start something going
inspire *vb.* to cause someone to have an emotion or do something

L

lethal *adj.* deadly; able to cause death
livestock *n.* farm animals such as sheep, cattle, and pigs
loot *vb.* to steal things in a situation of confusion

M

mainstream *adj.* matching the attitudes and values of most people in society
maintain *vb.* to keep something in the same condition or at the same level
metabolism *n.* the chemical processes that use food and water to help the body grow, heal and make energy
migrate *vb.* to move from area to another according to time of year
monitor *vb.* to keep track of something for a specific purpose

N

navigate *vb.* to find a path to get somewhere

O

obesity *n.* the condition of being very overweight
organism *n.* living animal or plant

P

passive *adj.* not active; allowing things to happen without trying to make changes
peak *vb.* to reach the highest level
predator *n.* animal that lives by killing and eating other animals
principal *adj.* main; most important
prolonged *adj.* continuing for a long time; lengthy

R

radical *adj.* very new or different from what is usual or traditional
rapidly *adv.* quickly
reclaimed *adj.* useful again or in a desirable condition again
remains *n.* corpse; what is left of a dead body
replenish *vb.* to refill; to make full again
reservoir *n.* large man-made lake where water is stored

S

scorn *n.* a feeling of strong disrespect mixed with anger
scrutinize *vb.* to examine carefully
sedentary *adj.* not physically active
seductive *adj.* tempting; very attractive
seedy *adj.* not respectable or decent
seep *vb.* to flow slowly through small openings
severe *adj.* serious or very bad
shadow *vb.* to follow and watch in a secret way
shatter *vb.* to break into many small pieces
sludge *n.* thick, muddy substance
sound *adj.* sensible or practical
species *n.* a group of animals or plants with common characteristics
status symbol *n.* something that shows a person's high level in society
steep *adj.* very high
stranded *adj.* left in a place with no way to leave
stringent *adj.* strict or serious
sufficient *adj.* enough to fill a need
surge *n.* a sudden big increase
surplus *n.* an amount that is extra or left over
susceptible *adj.* easily affected or harmed by something

T

timid *adj.* shy
trace *n.* a very tiny amount
transition *n.* change from one condition or situation to another
treacherous *adj.* full of dangers
trespass *vb.* to go on private property without permission

U

underestimate *vb.* to believe something is less in size, amount or quality
underground *adj.* separate or hidden from the main part of society
underrated *adj.* having too low a value put on

V

vandalism *n.* the act of damaging property on purpose
vast *adj.* huge in size, amount, degree or range
vegetation *n.* plant life
ventilated *adj.* letting in fresh air
vicinity *n.* an area close to or around a place
vigilant *adj.* alert and watchful
vital *adj.* very important
vulnerable *adj.* open to danger, attack or harm

W

widespread *adj.* common over a huge area or among many people

Answer Key

Lesson 1 Heatstroke
A 1.b, 2.c, 3.b, 4.c, 5.b, 6.c
B 1.b, 2.c, 3.c, 4.b, 5.c, 6.c
E 2. undercook 3. underemployed 4. underage 5. undercharged 6. underpaid

Lesson 2 Whales on the Beach
A 1.b, 2.c, 3.b, 4.c, 5.a, 6.a
B 1.a, 2.b, 3.b, 4.c, 5.b, 6.b
E 2.a, 3.b, 4.c, 5.c, 6.a

Lesson 3 Lightning Strikes
A 1.b, 2.b, 3.c, 4.b, 5.a, 6.a
B 1.a, 2.b, 3.a, 4.c, 5.b, 6. c
E 2.b, 3.a, 4.e, 5.c

Lesson 4 Graffiti
A 1.a, 2.c, 3.a, 4.c, 5.a, 6.b
B 1.c, 2.a, 3.c, 4.b, 5.c, 6.c
E 2.a, 3.c, 4.b, 5.a, 6.a, 7.c steep:b

Lesson 5 Frostbite
A 1.c, 2.c, 3.b, 4.a, 5.b, 6.c
B 1.a, 2.b, 3.a, 4.c, 5.b, 6.c
E 2.a, 3.b, 4.d, 5.c, 6.a, 7.d

Lesson 6 Caribou
A 1.b, 2.a, 3.c, 4.c, 5.a, 6.b
B 1.a, 2.b, 3.c, 4.a, 5.a, 6.b
E 2.b, 3.a, 4.d, 5.e, 6.c, 7.e

Lesson 7 San Francisco Earthquake

A 1.b, 2.c, 3.c, 4.a, 5.c, 6.a

B 1.a, 2.b, 3.a, 4.a, 5.c, 6.c

E Student responses will vary.

Lesson 8 Chocolate

A 1.b, 2.a, 3.a, 4.c, 5.b, 6.b

B 1.b, 2.a, 3.c, 4.b, 5.a, 6.a

E Society A: a big scar, a medal of courage Society B: soft skin, being overweight Society C: a suntan, a long vacation in Mexico

Lesson 9 Food Allergies

A 1.c, 2.b, 3.c, 4.a, 5.a, 6.a

B 1.a, 2.b, 3.b, 4.a, 5.a, 6.c

E 2.d, 3.a, 4.b, 5.c, rapid: b, a

Lesson 10 Polar Bears

A 1.b, 2.c, 3.a, 4.b, 5.a, 6.c

B 1.c, 2.b, 3.b, 4.c, 5.b, 6.c

E 2. inhospitable, bad 3. a tragedy, sad 4. tired, exhausted 5. harsh, negative

Lesson 11 Global Warming

A 1.a, 2.c, 3.b, 4.c, 5.a, 6.c

B 1.b, 2.a, 3.b, 4.b, 5.b, 6.c

E 2. main 3. seems limitless 4. make easier to cope with 5. slowly increased

Lesson 12 Extreme Sports

A 1.a, 2.a, 3.a, 4.b, 5.c, 6.b

B 1.c, 2.c, 3.b, 4.c, 5.c, 6.a

E Student responses will vary.

Lesson 13 Alzheimer's Disease

A 1.b, 2.c, 3.c, 4.b, 5.a, 6.a

B 1.b, 2.a, 3.c, 4.b, 5.a, 6.a

E 2. common among people everywhere 3. makes weaker 4. not traditional
5. goes along with everything 6. examining the inside of a dead body

Lesson 14 An Australian Pest

A 1.a, 2.c, 3.b, 4.c, 5.a, 6.b

B 1.b, 2.b, 3.a, 4.a, 5.a, 6.a

E Preferred choices: people who are between jobs, Inuit, senior citizens, new Canadians, homemaker, employer

Lesson 15 Sydney Tar Ponds

A 1.c, 2.b, 3.a, 4.a, 5.c, 6.a

B 1.b, 2.a, 3.a, 4.b, 5.b, 6.a

E 2. polluted 3. contaminated, contamination 4. pollute 5. Pollution 6. contaminate

Lesson 16 Identity Theft

A 1.a, 2.b, 3.a, 4.c, 5.a, 6.a

B 1.c, 2.a, 3.c, 4.a, 5.b, 6.b

E 2. angry, livid 3. enormous, big 4. depressed, sad 5. scalding, hot
6. terrified, scared

Lesson 17 Diabetes

A 1.b, 2.a, 3.a, 4.c, 5.b, 6.b

B 1.c, 2.b, 3.b, 4.c, 5.a, 6.c

E 2.c, 3.a, 4.c, 5.d, 6.b, 7.a, 8.b

Lesson 18 Greyhound Racing

A 1.a, 2.b, 3.a, 4.b, 5.b, 6.c
B 1.b, 2.b, 3.c, 4.b, 5.c, 6.b
E 2. mean 3. letting in fresh air 4. a hard thing to cope with 5. not promising 6. easy to train

Lesson 19 Water

A 1.b, 2.a, 3.c, 4.c, 5.a, 6.b
B 1.a, 2.c, 3.c, 4.c, 5.b, 6.a
E 2.b, 3.a/e, 4.c, 5.e, 6.d, 7.c, c

Lesson 20 Body Piercing

A 1.a, 2.b, 3.a, 4.b, 5.c, 6.c
B 1.a, 2.c, 3.c, 4.c, 5.a, 6.a
E 1. The main stream is the biggest part of the water system. Mainstream music is enjoyed by a big part of society. 2. Stars in the sky shine bright and can be seen by everyone. Music video stars are famous and seen by many people. 3. In the dark means not knowing what is going on because the meaning is hidden from you. When you are in the dark, there is no light so things are hidden from you. 4. A neck made of rubber can be stretched. Rubbernecking means stretching your neck so you can get a clearer view of something.

Word Search Answers

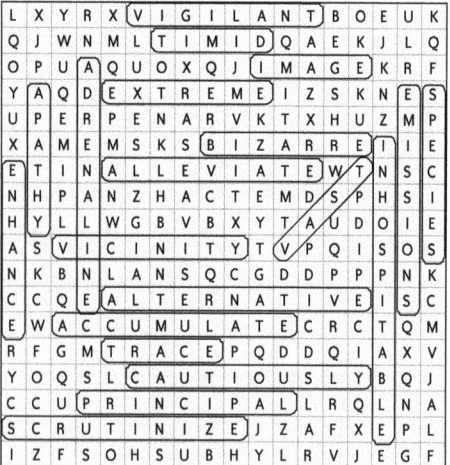

Word Search 1

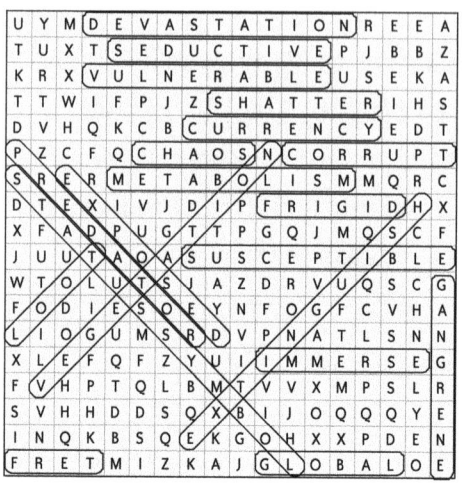

Word Search 2

Word Search 3

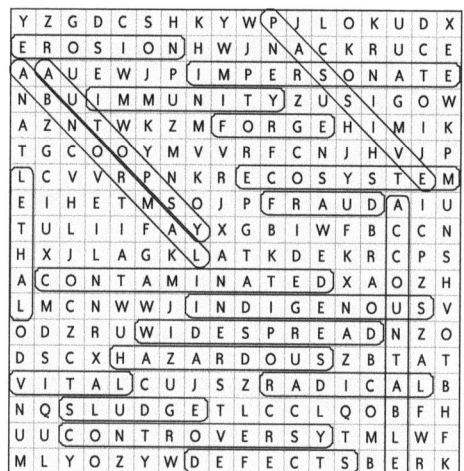

Word Search 4

Word Search 5

www.ingramcontent.com/pod-product-compliance
Ingram Content Group UK Ltd.
Pitfield, Milton Keynes, MK11 3LW, UK
UKHW051653180426
11947UKWH00021B/1926